WORKBOOK

How to Find Relationships That Are Good for You

SAFE PEOPLE

and Avoid Those That Aren't

DR. HENRY CLOUD
DR. JOHN TOWNSEND

WITH LISA GUEST

ZONDERVAN

Safe People Workbook
Copyright © 1995 by Henry Cloud and John Townsend

Requests for information should be addressed to:

Zondervan, 3900 *Sparks Dr. SE, Grand Rapids, Michigan 49546*

ISBN 978-0-310-49501-7

Published in association with Yates & Yates, www.yates2.com.

Printed in the United States of America

HB 08.16.2023

SAFE PEOPLE

PEOPLE

WORKBOOK

Resources by Henry Cloud and John Townsend

Books

Boundaries (and workbook)
Boundaries in Dating (and workbook)
Boundaries in Marriage (and workbook)
Boundaries with Kids (and workbook)
Boundaries with Teens (Townsend)
Changes That Heal (and workbook) (Cloud)
Hiding from Love (Townsend)
How People Grow (and workbook)
How to Have That Difficult Conversation You've Been Avoiding
Making Small Groups Work
The Mom Factor (and workbook)
Raising Great Kids
Raising Great Kids Workbook for Parents of Preschoolers
Raising Great Kids Workbook for Parents of School-Age Children
Raising Great Kids Workbook for Parents of Teenagers
Safe People (and workbook)
12 "Christian" Beliefs That Can Drive You Crazy

Video Curriculum

Boundaries
Boundaries in Dating
Boundaries in Marriage
Boundaries with Kids
Raising Great Kids for Parents of Preschoolers
ReGroup (with Bill Donahue)

Audio

Boundaries
Boundaries in Dating
Boundaries in Marriage
Boundaries with Kids
Boundaries with Teens (Townsend)
Changes That Heal (Cloud)
How People Grow
How to Have That Difficult Conversation You've Been Avoiding
Making Small Groups Work
The Mom Factor
Raising Great Kids

CONTENTS

INTRODUCTION

Is your ability to pick out a good car better than your ability to pick a good friend? It needn't be that way. Character discernment is a skill that can be learned and sharpened. In fact, this skill is key to our personal and spiritual growth because God uses the people in our lives to make each of us the person he wants us to be.

What is character discernment? It is simply being able to tell the sheep from the goats in your life, being able to evaluate who is good for you and who isn't. Those who are good for us we call "safe people," and these individuals truly make us better people by their presence in our lives.

The Bible contains the keys to developing the skill of character discernment. God's Word helps us understand how to tell safe people from unsafe ones. It also teaches us how to become a safe person for others. In this age of broken relationships, these scriptural principles are both timeless and timely.

Just as you did when you read the book, as you work through this study guide you will look outside yourself as well as inside. This guide is designed to help you critically evaluate the people in whom you are investing yourself. The scriptural principles outlined will help you see the true nature of others, both good and bad.

This guide will also help you look inside yourself and identify your blind spots and vulnerabilities and understand why you are easy prey to manipulative people or susceptible to controlling individuals. Besides gaining an awareness of your weaknesses, you'll learn how to mature past them. You'll also look at yourself to see how you may be unsafe for others.

Finally, as you read this guide to safe people, we pray that you will sense God's impassioned concern for you. May the promise of Philippians 1:6—"He who began a good work in you will carry it on to completion until the day of Christ Jesus"—truly be a source of confidence and encouragement as you learn to enter more fully and freely the world of relationship with God and with those safe people who represent him.

HENRY CLOUD, PH.D.
JOHN TOWNSEND, PH.D.

PART ONE

Unsafe People

CHAPTER ONE

What Is an Unsafe Person?

In retrospect, I (John) can see all the reasons why Karen was an unsafe person. But while we were dating, I was caught up in the wonder and excitement of the relationship with her and missed a few things along the way. Even after the relationship ended so abruptly, I wondered for years how I could have been so wrong about thinking someone was so right (p. 19).*

IS THIS YOUR LIFE?

The lessons I learned in the romantic sphere can be learned from any relationship because we can be wrong about thinking someone is right in a variety of situations (p. 19).

- Think about the relationship(s) that came to mind as you read about my relationship with Karen. Who has been a Karen in your life?

  - A romantic interest
  - A best friend
  - A coworker
  - A relative
  - A church acquaintance
  - Other:

- Have you had more than one Karen in your life?

---

*The parts in italics are summaries of the book *Safe People*. Page references are in parentheses.

- Have you blamed yourself when you've been hurt by the Karen(s) in your life? If so, for what did you blame yourself?

- How have you answered the question you've probably asked yourself—"What in the world am I doing wrong?"

CHARACTER DISCERNMENT

What are you doing wrong in relationships? The answer to that question probably lies in the fact that you are untrained in discerning the character of people. Without the proper maturity and skills, our God-given need for support and attachment to others (Gen. 2:18) can get us into real trouble (p. 19).

When I (Henry) asked a group of college students, "What qualities do you look for in a potential date or mate?" they gave broad religious answers to my question—"I want someone spiritual, godly, ambitious, fun to be with," etc.—but people having trouble in a relationship don't identify broad religious issues as the problem (p. 20).

- What have you heard hurting friends complain about regarding their relationships?

- What have you said when you've talked about relationships you've been in that haven't worked out?

When God talks about his problem relationships, he talks about people being "far away" (Matt. 15:8 NASB), "unfaithful" (Josh. 22:16 NASB), "proud" (Deut. 8:14; Ps. 36:2), "unloving" (1 John 4:20), or "judgmental" (Rom. 2:1). In short, God looks at character. We tend to look on the outside and not the inside of a person (1 Sam. 16:7; Matt. 23:25–28).

So we choose people based on outward appearance, but then we experience the inside of them and come up empty-handed (pp. 20–21).

- In the past, what have you looked at when you've entered into a relationship with someone?

- Think of a specific time when the inside was radically and painfully different from the outside of the person with whom you were in relationship. List the positive outside qualities and the painful inside ones.

WHO ARE THE BAD GUYS?

In real life, the bad guys aren't as easy to identify as those on Saturday morning cartoons. Unsafe people are particularly difficult to spot, but many unsafe people fall under three categories: the abandoners, the critics, and the irresponsibles (p. 21).

Abandoners *start a relationship but can't finish it. Often, abandoners have been abandoned themselves. Sometimes, afraid of intimacy, they prefer shallow acquaintances. Others are looking for perfect friends, and they leave when the cracks start showing (pp. 21–22).*

- Have you, like Ron, been drawn to abandoners? What reasons have been behind the abandonment—their own history of being abandoned, their fear of true closeness, and/or their search for perfect friends?

- Do you tend to be an abandoner? Which of the three reasons contribute to your abandoning behavior?

Critics take a parental role with everyone they know. More concerned with confronting errors than making connections, critics are judgmental, speak the truth without love, and have no room for grace or forgiveness (pp. 22–23).

- Have you, like Martha, been drawn to critics? What might be behind this uncanny attraction?

- Do you tend to be a critic? Why do you think you tend to point the finger away from rather than at yourself?

Irresponsibles don't take care of themselves or others. They have problems with delaying gratification, they don't consider the consequences of their actions, and they don't follow through on their commitments. They're like grown-up children. They can't be depended on to do what they say (pp. 23–24).

- Do you have a Jeremy in your life or have you in the past? (See the checklist on page 24.) Are you continuing to be an enabler or have you dealt constructively with that Jeremy?

- Do you tend to be an irresponsible? Do you have a hard time on follow-through when, with good intentions, you say you'll do something? Are you always in financial straits? Do you have a hard time considering, much less planning for, tomorrow? Do you struggle with delayed gratification? Where do you think you learned this behavior and why do you think you continue it?

Looking at these three types of unsafe people—abandoners, critics, and irresponsibles—may help you see your present support system (and yourself!) more realistically. In the following chapters, we'll contrast more specific character traits of unsafe people

with the godly character traits of safe people so that you'll be able to look for danger sig-
nals in your relationships—and then learn to make wise decisions about how to handle
the unsafe people in your life (p. 25).

— *Prayer* —

Father God, I already see how I choose people based more on their outward appearance than on the kind of character traits you look for. That new perspective helps me
understand why it can be such a painful surprise when I experience the inside of
those people. I ask you to help me, as I work through this guide, to become more discerning of the inside. Even now, Lord, help me see where I am in relationship with an
abandoner, a critic, or an irresponsible. Show me, too, God, where I am the abandoner, critic, or irresponsible in a relationship. And then show me what to do in both
situations. I pray in Jesus' name. Amen.

CHAPTER TWO

Personal Traits of Unsafe People

❧

As Mary learned the hard way, unsafe people have personal traits that make them extremely dangerous. They act is if they "have it all together." They are self-righteous. They demand trust. And when their facade of perfection is stripped away, they blow up (as Donna did) or disappear (p. 27).

In this chapter, we'll look at eleven personal traits of unsafe people; the next chapter details nine interpersonal traits of unsafe people. Keep in mind that these negative traits have corresponding positive ones that, together, will give you a good working definition of a safe person. Also, keep in prayer those relationships in which you observe the warning signal of any of these traits of an unsafe person (p. 28).

1. Unsafe people think they "have it all together" instead of admitting their weaknesses (pp. 28–29).

- Why does the attitude of "having it all together" make a person unsafe?

- Sally found herself cast in the role of the "weak" one in her relationship with Julia, and she didn't feel like Julia needed her. What have you felt in such a relationship with an unsafe person? Beside each answer you circle, note how the person's actions, attitudes, and/or words contributed to your feelings.

  - Disconnected
  - "One down"
  - Weaker than you actually are

17

- Dependent on the "strong one"
- Angry and hostile toward the "together" one
- The need to compete to reverse the role

- *When we feel weak in a relationship, we may try to be strong in another and end up with several imbalanced, unsafe relationships (p. 29).* What can we do to balance the elements of strength and weakness in a relationship?

- Are you casting yourself in the role of the "strong" one in your relationships? How are you benefiting from that role? How are you suffering?

- *When we pretend to "have it all together" rather than admit our weaknesses, we inhibit our spiritual and emotional growth. Such growth comes, in part, when we confess our faults and weaknesses to each other (Eccl. 4:10; James 5:16) (p. 29).* What have you experienced when you've been able to confess a fault, weakness, or sin to another person? What is keeping you from doing so and therefore keeping you from growing?

2. Unsafe people are religious instead of spiritual (pp. 29–30).

- Explain the difference between being religious and being spiritual. Comment, for instance, on the issues of honesty, integrity, and being "real."

- Why does being religious instead of spiritual make a person unsafe?

- *Becoming more and more "religious" can mean losing touch with our vulnerability, our pain, our need for other people, our sinfulness and "bad parts," and many other aspects of what it means to be a person (p. 29).* What areas of yourself are you perhaps losing touch with as you become "religious"?

- Why is a person who has lost touch with his or her vulnerability, pain, need for other people, and sinfulness a dangerous person?

- How have you benefited from relationships with spiritual people—people who really know God, who are able to understand and love others, and who are honest about themselves and about life?

- What are you doing to become more spiritual, to truly know God and his ways, instead of merely filling your talk with a lot of religious language and your life with religious activities?

3. Unsafe people are defensive instead of open to feedback (pp. 30–31).

- Why does defensiveness make a person unsafe?

- Are you more like Jay or my (Henry) other friend when it comes to reacting to feedback? Give an example or two.

- What do you do about confronting the Jays in your life? How have you been hurt by such people who do not own their need to change and who lash out when they are confronted?

- What have you learned from confronting those people in your life who, like my other friend, are more interested in doing what is right than in appearing "right" in their own eyes?

- According to Proverbs 9:7–9, how does an unsafe person ("a mocker") respond to confrontation and rebuke? How does a safe ("wise") person respond?

- What have you learned about yourself from other people's rebukes (Matt. 18:15)? How have you grown as a result?

4. Unsafe people are self-righteous instead of humble (pp. 31–32).

- Why does self-righteousness make a person unsafe? What are the consequences of being in relationship with a self-righteous person? Think about your own experiences.

- Do you tend to be more like the Pharisee or the tax collector in Jesus' parable (Luke 18:10–14)? Talk about that side of yourself.

- In what relationships are you self-righteous like the Pharisee? How satisfying are those relationships?

- *Seeing ourselves as good and others as bad (being self-righteous instead of humble) is a "not me" experience: we don't allow ourselves to see certain realities as part of ourselves (p. 32).* Do you have such a perspective on sin? Do you talk about people "in the world" as if you are unable to identify with them? What does the scene from Isaiah 6:1–5 and the truth of Romans 3:23 say to you?

5. Unsafe people only apologize instead of changing their behavior (pp. 32–34).

- Why does only apologizing rather than changing one's behavior make a person unsafe?

- Explain the difference between apologizing and repenting. The words of John the Baptist in Luke 3:7–9 can guide your answer.

- What have you learned from relationships with people who merely apologize, from people who are more sorry about getting caught than about not being the kind of person God would have them be?

- What have you learned from relationships with people who truly repent, motivated by a hunger and thirst for righteousness and a love for the injured party?

- Do you only apologize or do you, like that well-known Christian leader, apologize and change? What motivates your behavior?

6. Unsafe people avoid working on their problems instead of dealing with them (p. 34).

- What benefits come from dealing with our problems?

- Why does the tendency to avoid working on one's problems make a person unsafe?

- Are you reluctant to admit and work on your problems? Or have you learned to take responsibility for your life and to share your problems with others so that both you and they can grow? Talk about why.

7. Unsafe people demand trust instead of earning it (pp. 35–36).

- Who is demanding trust from you? Who gets defensive and angry when you question their actions? Why is this person unsafe?

- In John 10:37–38, what does Jesus, who is completely trustworthy, teach us about whether we should trust him—and about trust in general?

- What benefits come with being open to learning from people who love us enough to tell us when we are unknowingly doing something wrong (Ps. 139:23–24)?

- Are you, like Jesus, comfortable when people you care about "audit" you? Or do you demand to be trusted without earning that trust? Comment on how you got to be the way you are.

8. Unsafe people believe they are perfect instead of admitting their faults (p. 36).

- Why is a person who believes he or she is perfect an unsafe person?

- Explain why love "depends in part on our ability to own and share our faults." Luke 7:36–47—especially Jesus' words in verse 47—may help.

- Are you still striving to be perfect? If so, why? If not, what has happened in your life to help you learn to acknowledge your humanness and internalize the grace of being loved even though you're not perfect?

9. Unsafe people blame others instead of taking responsibility (pp. 36–37).

- Why is a person who doesn't take responsibility for himself or herself an unsafe person?

- What personal problems and character issues are you blaming others for instead of taking responsibility for? Why are you choosing that route?

- Or what hard work are you doing as you take responsibility for your problems and character issues? What fruits of your labor are you seeing at this time?

10. Unsafe people lie instead of telling the truth (pp. 37–38).

- Why do deception and dishonesty make a person unsafe?

- When have you been hurt by someone deceiving you? What early warning signs did you miss that you might see now?

- What is your perspective on the lies you tell? Are they a strategy by which you manage your life and relationships? Why have you adopted this strategy?

• Or, seeing your lies as a problem to change, have you been open to confrontation and repentance? What personal growth have you experienced as a result of your openness to the truth? How have your relationships benefited from your commitment to telling the truth?

11. Unsafe people are stagnant instead of growing (p. 38).

• Some people don't see their own problems; they are rigidly fixed and not subject to growth (Prov. 17:10) (p. 38). Why are such stagnant people unsafe?

• Are you blind to your own problems? What will you do to overcome that blindness?

• Or are you aware of your problems and desire to mature and grow? In what area of your life or character are you aware of some growth?

Remember that no one is perfect. Even safe people—who are sinners, too—will at times stumble and be unsafe. So, when you are evaluating someone's character, look at these eleven traits in terms of degree. If a person seems willing to change, forgive that person graciously and work with him or her. But if he or she resists you, proceed with caution (pp. 38–39).

— *Prayer* —

Father God, thank you for what you are teaching me about people—and, at the same time, about myself and the kind of person you want me to be. You know the hurts I've experienced and you know how looking for these eleven personal traits can help me avoid being hurt again.

Lord, give me a discerning spirit—but not a harshly critical one—as I look out for people who "have it all together"; who are religious, defensive, and self-righteous; who apologize freely but don't make any attempt to change; who avoid working on their problems, demand to be trusted, believe they are perfect, blame others, lie, and are stagnant.

And, Lord, be at work in my life to help me be more able to admit my weaknesses. Help me become truly spiritual, genuine in my knowledge of you, confrontable, and humble. Help me be willing to change my behavior when I see that I'm wrong and teach me to deal with my problems rather than blame other people. Help me also to be willing to earn people's trust, admit my faults, take responsibility for my life, and tell the truth. Lord, be at work in my life so that I will grow to be the person you want me to be. I pray in Jesus' name. Amen.

CHAPTER THREE

Interpersonal Traits of Unsafe People

_____

In the last chapter, we learned eleven personal traits of unsafe people. Now we'll look at nine interpersonal traits of unsafe people. Personal traits describe who we are. Interpersonal traits describe how we connect—how we operate in relationships, how we move close or pull away, and how we build up or destroy. Let this chapter help you examine the people in your life and see more clearly the difference between the safe and the unsafe ones (p. 41).

1. Unsafe people avoid closeness instead of connecting (pp. 41–43).

- *Intimacy occurs when we are open, vulnerable, and honest, able to share our real feelings, fears, failures, and hurts (p. 41).* With whom are you able to be intimate? What growth and joy come from this/these relationship(s)?

- Is there a Wayne in your life? Are you now in—or have you ever been in—a long-term relationship in which you haven't gotten to really know the other person? What feelings did this relationship cause in you? What makes/made this person unsafe?

- *If you are currently uneasy about a relationship, ask yourself, "Does this relation-ship breed more togetherness or more isolation within me?" Then, if you're feeling alone in the relationship, ask yourself if your sense of detachment may be from some block inside of you (p. 43).* What will you do to explore and resolve that blockage? If your sense of detachment comes because of who the other person is, what will you do about the relationship?

2. Unsafe people are only concerned about "I" instead of "we" (pp. 43–45).

- Have you known a Barry, someone for whom you served as an audience for his conversation with himself? How did that "relationship" make you feel? Why was that person unsafe?

- *Safe people are empathic. If unsafe people are self-centered, safe people are rela-tionship-centered, and that priority shows itself in the all-important action of empa-thy (p. 44).* How do you define empathy? How does empathy make a relationship safe? How does a safe person reveal his or her empathic nature?

- Would you describe yourself as more self-centered or more relationship-centered and empathic? If the former, why do you think you are that way—and what will you do to change? If the latter, how do you reveal your empathy in your rela-tionships?

- What does Jesus teach about empathy in Matthew 7:12, the Golden Rule? How does empathy create love?

- *Safe people selflessly act on their empathy (p. 45).* When, if ever, has someone helped you (been empathic) only to exploit that help for his or her own gain later? When have you been a chronic "giver" in a relationship? Are you being a chronic "taker" in any relationship?

- *Love seeks the good of the other: it is "not self-seeking" (1 Cor. 13:5) (p. 45).* Who in your life has made genuine concern for you known through selfless concrete actions? Be specific—and thank God for that person!

3. Unsafe people resist freedom instead of encouraging it (pp. 46–48).

- Have you ever known a Brian, someone who had a hard time hearing no from you? Why is such a person unsafe?

- Do you struggle when someone says no to you? If so, what do you think lies behind that?

- *Love protects the separateness of the other. Separate, safe people take responsibility for what is theirs—and they don't take ownership of what isn't theirs (Gal. 6:1–5) (pp. 46–47).* Why does love wither and die without such separateness?

- *The opposite of separateness is enmeshment. In an enmeshing relationship, one person feels threatened by the other's individuality and seeks to control him. Safe people, however, encourage, value, and nurture the separateness of other people (p. 47).* Are you able to encourage, value, and nurture the separateness of other people? How do you—or how would you—benefit from doing so?

- Comment on your ability to say no. How did you learn that skill? What safe people in your life taught you that it was okay to say no, to be a separate person? If you're still learning this skill, with whom can you test the waters? With whom will you risk being separate by saying no, disagreeing, or choosing a value, event, or emotion distinct from his or hers?

4. Unsafe people flatter us instead of confronting us (pp. 48–49).

- Who has been a Crystal in your life? Who liked stroking you but avoided confronting you? Who could be positive but not directly negative? Why is a Crystal unsafe?

- With whom are you a Crystal? How does your being a Crystal keep truth, righteousness, and honesty out of that relationship?

- When has someone loved you enough to confront you about your sin, selfishness, or denial just as Jesus confronted the churches about what he held against them (Rev. 2:4, 14, 20)? How did you feel at the time? What have you come to appreciate about those humbling, hurtful—but not harmful—words?

- Who in your life would benefit today from genuine, heartfelt, truth-based praise (Prov. 27:2)? Offer it!

- *Praise affirms truth, but stroking avoids the truth by exclusively praising (p. 49).* Now ask yourself: With whom do I need to be a confronter, not merely a stroker? Be prayerful about the confrontation so that you speak the truth safely and in love, not as a critical parent.

- Who in your life seems to tell you only your good points? Beware! *They aren't loving you enough to tell you when your attitude or behavior is driving your life over a cliff—even though you desperately need to know it (p. 49)!*

5. Unsafe people condemn us instead of forgiving us (pp. 49–51).

- *Forgiveness makes it possible for love to "bear all things, believe all things, hope all things, endure all things" (1 Cor. 13:7 NASB) (pp.49–50).* Why is such forgiveness fundamental to a safe relationship? Why does the absence of forgiveness make a person unsafe?

- When has someone forgiven you for hurting her or letting her down? What did this experience teach you about God? How did receiving forgiveness produce growth in you?

- *God, the ultimate Forgiver, openly confronts us and clearly shows us how we wound him (Ezek. 6:9) (p. 50).* Should people who can forgive also be—like God—able to confront?

- *A safe person who confronts and forgives us loves us with a love that helps heal and transform us into the person God intends us to be (p. 50).* In sharp contrast, how has condemnation from a person unable to forgive you affected you and even blocked your growth?

- Are you able to forgive and, ideally, able to confront? Ask God to continue to enable you to speak the truth in love and to extend to others the kind of forgiveness he extends to you.

- Or are you more often a condemner, one who identifies weaknesses, focuses on failures, and won't let go of the past? What will you do with this realization about yourself?

6. Unsafe people stay in parent/child roles instead of relating as equals (pp. 51–54).

- Why is someone who resists your adult functioning and who reacts to your adultness by withdrawing from it an unsafe person?

- Who in your life rejoices as you develop and use your God-given gifts and talents and applauds your growing up and maturing? What benefits do you derive from your relationship with this safe person?

- If you are a parent, explain what the instruction in Proverbs 22:6 means — "Train a child in the way he should go, and when he is old he will not turn from it." What do safe people do in response to this instruction?

- *"I feel like a kid around them"* is one reaction to unsafe people (p. 52). Around whom do you feel like a kid? Who in your life has assumed a parental role? How do you deal with this person's criticism and unwanted guidance? Now ask yourself, "Whom might I make feel like a kid?" Which of your actions or words might contribute to that person's feelings? Why do you think you are making that person feel like a child?

- *"I feel like I have to be their parent" (p. 53).* Who wants you to be their parent? With whom in your life (someone over eighteen years of age who is not under your legal guardianship) have you assumed a parental role? Has this person cast you as the approval-providing parent or the authoritarian controller? How do you deal with this role as parent? Now ask yourself, "Whom have I cast as a parent in my life?" Why are you doing this?

- *"I feel equal with them" (p. 53).* Who in your life doesn't make you become either a child or a parent? How do you benefit from this person who seeks first God's kingdom on his own (Matt. 6:33), perhaps wanting your counsel but not needing your approval—this person who wants you to flourish in your life even though you may not have his approval? Now ask yourself, "Whose growth am I encouraging and applauding?" How are you doing this? How are you benefiting from this relationship?

- What have you learned about the kind of friend you tend to be? What will you do to more actively work for your friends' growth? What will you do about any tendency you've noticed to keep a person in a child's role or cast a person in a parent's role?

7. Unsafe people are unstable over time instead of being consistent (pp. 54–56).

- Why does being unstable over time make a person unsafe?

- When in your life have you seen time be the best judge of character? What did you learn and how did you learn that lesson?

- Do you have a Bernard in your life? How do you deal with him? Or are you a Bernard? Where have you seen yourself in this description? What will you do with this insight about yourself?

- Do you have a Pamela in your life? How has she passed the time test? Are you a Pamela for your friends? For whom does your relationship mean that you're there for good?

- *Safe, time-friendly people tend to make fewer emotional commitments than a Bernard does. They live up to their commitments to their friends. They keep promises they make, and they say no when they can't make a promise. Their love is abiding, timeless, and unchanging, just like its Author (Heb. 13:8) (p. 56).* Having read this description, what will you do to be a safer, more consistent person?

8. Unsafe people are a negative influence, rather than a positive one (pp. 56–58).

- Why does being a negative influence make a person unsafe?

- Has there been a Harry in your life? What negative traits did that person bring out in you? What happened to help you realize this person's negative influence?

- Remember the example of the woman who is swept off her feet by an insincere charmer? What good things may result from her feeling loved? What bad will ultimately happen?

- *Safe people are not perfect, but they help us progress toward Christlike character by helping us be more loving, more honest, more forgiving, and more mutual. Safe people make us better people for being around them (Luke 6:43; 1 Cor. 15:33), and good company builds up our hearts (p. 57).* Who in your life comes to mind as you read this sentence? Thank God for their presence in your life.

- To whom can you go in order to help you determine whether a relationship is good for you? What relationship(s) do you have your doubts about? How are those relationships changing your life—for better or worse?

9. Unsafe people gossip instead of keeping secrets (pp. 58–59).

- Why is a gossip an unsafe person?

- *If you have ever entrusted part of yourself to another, and then heard about it from a third party, you have been triangulated (p. 58).* When has this happened to you? Is the triangulator still a part of your life? Do you trust that person now? Why or why not?

- *Often, a triangulator will attempt to justify his untrustworthiness by offering excuses such as "It just slipped out," or "It was for your own good" (p. 58).* What may lie beneath the gossip's excuses?

- Why is George Whitefield a good example of a safe person? Whom do you trust with your secrets? How has opening your soul's deep places and sharing them with another person strengthened your relationship? What has it done for your personal growth?

At this point in the study, you've gained some understanding about who's safe and who isn't—but don't stop here. The reason is that, even with this road map of character, you will probably still choose unsafe people. That's because the problem—as questions in this study guide have suggested—is often inside us.

We have needs, conflicts, and misperceptions that drive us toward unsafe people. And, until we address them, we'll continue seeking unsafe people "as a dog returns to its vomit" (Prov. 26:11). So, to best deal with unsafe people, we first need to understand what causes us to be unsafe. As the next chapter explains, unsafety finds its origin in sin—and sin is everyone's problem (Rom. 3:23) (p. 60).

— *Prayer* —

Father God, I understand that this road map isn't a guarantee that I'll be able to protect myself from unsafe people, but I thank you for what it has taught me. Help me look out for these eight interpersonal traits so that I can avoid being hurt.

Lord, again I ask that you give me a discerning spirit—but not a harshly critical one—as I look out for people who avoid closeness, who are more concerned about themselves than the relationship, who resist freedom, who flatter, who condemn, who stay in parent/child roles, who are unstable over time, and who are a negative influence on me.

And, Lord, I also ask that you be at work in my life to help me be more willing and able to connect with people and more concerned about the "we" and not the "I" in a relationship. Help me encourage freedom in my relationships. Give me the bold love I need to confront and not merely flatter. Teach me to forgive and to relate to the people in my life as equals, not as a parent or child. Help me to be consistent and reliable. And use me as a positive influence in the life of people I care about. I pray in Jesus' name. Amen.

CHAPTER FOUR

How We Lost Our Safety

———∿∿———

The lamp was broken, the cat was running away fast, and two preschoolers were frozen in position. That was the scene that precipitated Ricky's first lesson about unsafe people. He lost a little of his innocence that day as he began learning about the effects of the Fall (pp. 61–62).

THE SAD TRUTH

Most of us can relate to Ricky's experience. Like him, most of us have been surprised by unsafety (p. 62).

- When was the first time you were surprised by unsafety? How did you react? What do you remember feeling?

- Describe the most recent situation in which you were surprised by unsafety. How did you react? How has your reaction to unsafety in the world changed since you first recognized its existence?

GOD CREATED A SAFE WORLD

God never intended for us to suffer the effects of an unsafe world. Instead, he created a safe world, where Adam and Eve lived in harmony with him, each other, and themselves (p. 63).

- In John 17:21, what does Jesus pray that echoes God's concern for harmony between people, the harmony that comes when people are safe?

- What relationships have testified to you about God's safe love?

AND THEN CAME SIN . . .

Although created by God, our state of unity and harmonious relationship was not to be (p. 63).

Review Genesis 3:1–13.

- Summarize the events.

- What immediate evidence do you find here of disharmony between Adam and Eve? Between Adam and Eve and God?

- According to Genesis 3:14–19, what disharmony with the world would result from Adam and Eve's fall from grace?

Sin entered the world through Satan, Adam, and Eve, and it manifested itself in four areas: sin by us, sin against us, sin in the world, and Satan's strategies (p. 63).

SIN BY US

When we look at the different ways the Fall hurt our safety, the bad news is, some *of this is our fault. The good news is, not* all *of this is our fault. We all have a sinful nature that we inherited from Adam and Eve. When they gave in to the temptation to deny their humble dependence on God (Gen. 3:5), they damaged their relationship with God and with each other (p. 63).*

* What actions and aspects of your character do you think of when you hear the phrase "sinful nature"?

The sinful self does more than incline us to desire to do "bad things." The sinful self also makes us want to hurt others, be lazy, commit adultery, have a bad attitude, and so on. Our sinful nature is also our inclination to live without God. In our pride, we come to despise our dependency and powerlessness. Like Satan, we want to be the Creator, not the creature (Isa. 14:14) (p. 64).

* Now what actions and aspects of your character can you add to your list?

* When do you most despise your dependency?

* When have you given in to the temptation to live without God? What happened? What did you learn from that experience?

* How do you deal with your desire to live without God?

Besides inclining us to live without God, sin also set into play four more dynamics that are seriously destructive to our safety—and we'll look at each of those now (p. 64).

1. We are envious.

Envy makes us resent people who have something we don't have. When we envy, the very people who are loving, safe, and generous become the bad guys in our eyes. As Jesus' story about the workers illustrates (Matt. 20:1–16), envy makes generosity unfair. When we envy, we make the other person bad for not giving us what we need. Envy is the opposite of love, and envy spoils any chance to be loved. When we envy, we resent those who have something to offer us (pp. 64–66).

* When have you, like Paula and Margie, lost a friendship because of envy—yours or the other person's?

* What have you learned about envy from the text's discussion and this summary? What have you seen about yourself as you've read this description of envy?

* Explain how envy destroys safety.

* Do you tend to make the "haves" bad and the "have nots" good? Ask God to help you be grateful for what you have and to rejoice in the good things that others have.

2. We think we are self-sufficient.

God has created all of us incomplete, inadequate, and in need of a huge list of things we cannot provide for ourselves—things like God's love and provision, the love of other people, and our physical needs. Yet we desire to be a universe unto ourselves (pp. 66–67).

• What does the parable of the Pharisee and the tax collector (Luke 18:9–14) teach about the value of recognizing and confessing your needs?

• Think of a need you were finally able to admit. What brought you to that point? What positive things resulted from your admission that you are not self-sufficient?

• Explain how self-sufficiency ruins safety.

• Your needs are a gift from God and the cure to the sin of self-sufficiency. What will you do to make friends with your needs?

3. We think we are entitled to special treatment.

The sinful nature also causes a sense of entitlement. Not only did Satan envy God's goodness, not only did he wish to be self-sufficient, but he also felt he deserved privileged treatment (Isa. 14:14) (pp. 67–69).

• Look again at Jonah's reaction to God's mercy toward the people of Nineveh (Jonah 4:1–3). What does Jonah show you about how a sense of entitlement manifests itself? What feelings about himself and his people does Jonah's reaction suggest?

- How safe are the self-absorbed and grandiose people in your life, those people who feel entitled to special treatment?

- Explain why entitlement destroys safety.

- Perhaps you struggle with the sense that you are entitled to special treatment. The antidote is first asking forgiveness for your own imperfections. Do so now. Second, learn to forgive others for not meeting your outrageous expectations. Who is the first person you need to forgive? And what first step will you take?

4. We transgress against God's laws.

We violate boundaries God has set down. This aspect of our sinful nature rebels against having any restrictions. God had given Adam and Eve a lot of yeses. They had only one no, but they crossed that only limit he had set when they ate from the tree of the knowledge of good and evil (pp. 69–70).

- Think of a time when you chose to indulge self over loving God and obeying his commands (Ps. 19:13). What were the consequences of your decision? What did you learn from that experience?

- Explain why transgression destroys the safety in our relationships.

- When has someone's transgression destroyed the safety of your relationship with him or her?

- When has your transgression destroyed the safety of a relationship? Do you know what was behind your transgression?

Remember the teenager and the divorced single mother? They both drank, and both were responsible for their actions. But before they could be helped, they needed to understand why they were transgressing—and we need to understand that about ourselves. More often than not, isolation has caused the problem (p. 69).

> *Our sinful nature breeds envy, self-sufficiency, entitlement, and transgression.*
> *Envy, self-sufficiency, entitlement, and transgression breed isolation.*
> *Isolation breeds life problems (emotional, behavioral, relational) (p. 70).*

- Remember Randy, the man who turned to pornography because, he said, he wasn't in the Word enough? What did a closer look at Randy's life reveal about why he turned to pornography? Refer to the three points above.

- Now consider your own transgressions. What does a closer look at your life reveal about why you chose to violate God's boundaries? Again, refer to the three points above.

- What will you do with this new insight into yourself?

We are envious, we think we are self-sufficient, we think we are entitled to special treatment, and we transgress against God's laws. These are the sins by us that resulted from the Fall. Briefly summarize why they make people (ourselves included) unsafe (p. 70).

SIN AGAINST US

Having looked at our own fault first (Matt. 7:5), we can now move on to the other reasons we lose safety in this fallen world. The first of those reasons is that, since the Fall, we who are now sinful are also sinned against (p. 70).

In the fallen world, the innocent suffer for the evil of others (Matt. 18:6–7). And the innocent suffer because of love and its price tag. If love is free, then a lover is free to be unloving as well (p. 71).

- What suffering have you done because of the evil of others?

- What suffering have innocent people undergone because of your evil?

- Explain how sins against us destroy safety.

Sins against us may have affected our development in one or more of the following four ways (p. 71).

1. Our bonding process was disrupted.

Our first and deepest need as human beings is to bond, to attach to one another, to trust one another, to belong (pp. 71–72).

- The bonding process can be disrupted by detachment, abandonment, inconsistency, criticism, and abuse. Which, if any, disruptions did you encounter during your developmental years? Which of these sins against you have you experienced?

• How have those disruptions impacted your relationship with God? Your relationships with people? What else has resulted from your inability to bond? See the list on page 71 of the text.

• What have you done and/or what are you doing to deal with your unbondedness? What are you doing to recover your ability to be vulnerable, to be needy, and to trust?

2. Our boundaries were not respected.

Boundaries are our spiritual and emotional "property lines." They tell us where we end and where others begin. They help keep good things in us and bad things out. We take responsibility for what is ours, not for what isn't. We can carry our own loads, and we know when it's appropriate to help others with their burdens (Gal. 6:1–5).

Our boundaries—our ability to say no, to set limits, to establish consequences, and to not rescue others—can be injured by aggressive control, passive control, regressive control, and limitlessness (pp. 72–74).

• Which kinds of injuries to your boundaries—sins against you—have you experienced?

- Boundaryless people tend to feel abandoned when there is distance. They also tend to isolate as their only limit. What has your trouble with boundaries resulted in? See the symptoms on page 74 of the text.

- What have you done and/or what are you doing to learn to establish and maintain healthy boundaries?

3. We were not seen as whole people, with good and bad traits.

Coming to terms with our badness involves great loss and struggle for all of us—as the apostle Paul testifies when he cries, "For what I want to do I do not do, but what I hate I do" (Rom. 7:15). God's solution for resolving good-bad issues is a perfect God dying for a sinful people, a people who, like the prodigal son, don't have to be good to be loved (Luke 15:11–32). But many of us have learned that we are not loved when we are bad (pp. 74–76).

- We can learn that we are not loved when we are bad when we grow up with perfectionism, idealization, shaming, and splitting. Which of these lessons were you raised on? Which of these sins against you have you experienced?

- How have good-bad problems impacted your life? Has not being seen as both good *and* bad caused you to become a perfectionist? Are you able to forgive other people's sins? Your own sins? Can you accept other people's forgiveness? Do you keep your distance from people so they don't see your "bad side"? Do your ideals and your "shoulds" interfere with relationships? See the list on page 76 of the text for other ways good-bad problems affect us.

- What have you done and/or what are you doing to accept your whole self—the good *and* the bad—and to let that whole self be accepted by others?

4. We were not allowed to mature into adults.

Being an adult means taking our own roles in life; developing specialties and expertise in our jobs and careers; taking on our gender and sexuality roles; and coming to terms with what we believe about life, relationships, God, finances, and all the complex issues of life. Our need to become adults—to move from the child's one-down position to the equal and mutual position of being a grown-up—can be harmed by one-up relationships, one-down relationships, control, and criticism (pp. 76–78).

- Which of these sins against you did you experience?

When emerging adultness is disrupted, some people become compliant, others become controlling, and still others rebel. The adult-injured person is terrified of moving out of the child role. Even though they resent authority, they are afraid to challenge it (p. 77).

- How have you reacted to not being allowed to mature into an adult? See the list on page 78 of the text.

SIN IN THE WORLD

Many of our problems result from our own sin and that of others, but grave problems exist for which we really can't point a finger of blame. There is not a specific "perpetrator." The truth is that we live in a world that itself suffers the effects of the Fall (Rom. 8:21–22) (pp. 78–80).

- What situations come to mind when you read about "problems [that] exist for which we really can't point a finger of blame"? What evidence do you see around you that the world itself is suffering the effects of the Fall?

Young Chrissie's safety was challenged by death. We also lose a degree of safety through situations involving career moves and financial changes. Factors such as single parent homes and breakdowns in family structure contribute to safety loss. Genetic tendencies toward obesity and alcoholism reveal that our very make-up is corrupted by the Fall (p. 79).

- What events in your life have challenged your safety?

- What are you doing to take responsibility for the problems you've been dealt by and in this fallen world? What are you doing to put yourself in a position where God and his people can share your struggles and encourage you?

SATAN'S STRATEGIES

When we look at all the ways we have lost — and still lose — safety, it's easy to overlook our active and alive enemy, Satan, who works to keep us away from the safe relationships we so desperately need. He relies primarily on three tactics as he does his damage (p. 80).

Accusing: *Satan — whose very name means "accuser" — endlessly tries to separate God from us by reminding him (and often us!) of our guilt. God responds to those accusations by saying, "Yes, they sinned, but the penalty has been paid. They go free" (p. 80).*

- How do you respond to Satan's accusations?

- How can Satan's accusations about your guilt and sinfulness interfere with your efforts to establish and nurture relationships and keep you from finding safety?

Tempting: *Satan does more than merely influence people to do "bad things." He tempts us to get our needs met without relationship and without humility (pp. 80–81).*

- How do you respond when Satan tempts you with words like, "Why bother others? They'll see how weak you are. Where's your faith?"

- How can Satan's temptations to have you meet your own needs interfere with your efforts to establish and nurture relationships and keep you from finding safety?

Sifting: *Satan knows that the power of love is in relationship, so he delights in keeping people away from other people and from God. In fact, Satan asked permission to "sift you as wheat" (Luke 22:31), and "sifting" refers to splitting up, breaking up, or sorting out. He wants division so he can conquer (pp. 81–82).*

- When has Satan cleverly disguised his sifting behind such words and attitudes as "Get your act together before you come to church," or "If you had more faith, you wouldn't have this problem"? How did you respond? How would you respond today?

- How can Satan's sifting keep you from finding safety?

This chapter has given a four-part answer to the question, "How did I lose safety?" We have lost safety through sin by us, sin against us, sin in the world, and Satan's strategies. Become a student of yourself. Determine in which of these areas you have been most hurt and in what ways. Then begin working on the problems that have disconnected you. More than anything, God wants to have you fully reconciled with himself and his people (p. 82).

— *Prayer* —

Father God, as I think of those things that have robbed me of my safety—my own sin, sin against me, sin in the world, and Satan's strategies—I do wonder why I haven't lost even more! Thank you for your protection and your mercy. Thank you, too, for what you're helping me understand about myself, about you, about relationships, and about hurts and overcoming them.

Lord, open my eyes to my own sin and please be at work in me to transform me. Free me from envy, my attraction toward self-sufficiency, my sense that I'm entitled to special treatment, and my tendency to transgress against your laws. Open my eyes, too, to what lies beneath my patterns of transgression so that in you I may find freedom from those ways.

I also ask, God, that you would bring healing where I've been wounded by sins against me. You know how my bonding process was disrupted, how my boundaries were not respected, that I wasn't seen as a whole person with good *and* bad traits, and/or that I was not allowed to mature into an adult. Give me the courage and the strength to find the help I need.

Teach me, too, Lord, to take responsibility for what I'm dealing with as a result of the sin in the world. Guide me to safe people who can be vessels of encouragement and healing. And finally help me be aware of Satan's strategies—his accusing, his tempting, his sifting—so that I can stand strong in your power against him.

And thank you that, as I consider the overwhelming issues this chapter has addressed, I can find hope in the fact that, more than anything, you want me to be fully reconciled with you and with your people. May your will be done. I pray in Jesus' name. Amen.

PART TWO

Do I Attract
Unsafe People?

CHAPTER FIVE

Do I Have a "Safety Deficit"?

‑‑◁◁~

I can still see Lynn's thin, white legs pinwheeling crazily down the steep hill as, out of control, she headed toward a long stretch of barbed wire fencing. Fortunately, she was able to hear and respond to my father's instruction to turn. She veered to the side but then immediately caught her shoulder on the trunk of a large tree. I never thought we'd be thankful that Lynn ran into a tree—but we were (p. 85).

DO I HAVE ENOUGH SAFE PEOPLE IN MY LIFE?

People with unsafe connections are often out of control, like Lynn, but they don't have a tree to stop them. Instead, only sharp barbed wire waits—unsafe friends, who can badly hurt them if they run into them. What they need are friends who serve as stable trees that deflect them from disaster (Ps. 141:5) (p. 86).

- Have you in your past had more barbed wire fences than stable trees? Give some specific examples.

- When we exercise, a lack of water can mean the risk of dehydration. Likewise, the lack of attachment to people can mean real spiritual and emotional trouble. When has the lack of safe relationships resulted in spiritual and/or emotional trouble for you? What did you do to change that situation?

To determine whether you are safety-deficient now—to see if you are running low on safe people in your life—take an inventory of the following four areas of your life (p. 86).

Relationships: *The quality of our important friendships can tell us a great deal about how many barbed wire fences and how many stable trees are presently in our life (pp. 86–87).*

- Look again at the ten questions listed on pages 86 and 87 of the text and answer them if you haven't already.

- What does this list of questions tell you about yourself? Do you have some safety deficiencies in your life?

Functioning: *Now consider how well you are functioning at work, at home, and even in recreational activities. A drop in the level of functioning is often safety-related (pp. 87–88).*

- Which of the following signs of safety deficits do you see in yourself?

  - Monday blues that extend beyond Monday
  - Weekends without any soul-to-soul intimacy
  - Difficulty in completing tasks
  - Lapses in concentration
  - Inability to think creatively
  - Inability to take risks
  - Loss of energy
  - Motivation problems
  - Failure to achieve goals

- Explain why a lack of connection to people can contribute to each one of the items you circled.

Physical Health: Over the past few years, research has begun to affirm what Scriptures have been telling us for millennia: we don't have a body—we are a body. As the experiences of David and Jesus reflect (Ps. 6:2–3; Luke 22:44), our physical well-being is a good barometer of our emotional and spiritual life (pp. 88–90).

- What physical ailments have you experienced that may be related to stress and emotions?
  - Chronic headaches
  - Gastrointestinal problems
  - Back pain
  - Susceptibility to viruses
  - Weight issues
  - Other:

- Is your life more like Roseto many years ago, a town characterized by unusually solid and long-lasting personal relationships? Or is your life more like industrialized Roseto, a town of people moving on, new people moving in, and weak interpersonal connections? What does this analogy reveal to you or even warn you about?

Spiritual Life: A lack of safe people can wreak havoc in your personal relationship with God. In fact, your "relational condition" and your "spiritual condition" are as intricately connected as strands on a rope (pp. 90–91).

- As the apostle John points out, we often learn about the divine from the fleshly (1 John 4:20). What unsafe people in your life have contributed to an image of an unsafe God?

- What safe people in your life have helped you begin to believe that God may be safe?

- Now draw the two timelines described in the text (p. 90)—one that tracks your journey with God and identifies the stages you've experienced in your walk with him and the other that tracks your closest relationships. What parallels between the two journeys do you see? How did your relationships affect—both for good and bad—your perceptions of the Lord and therefore your walk with him?

It's important that we never evaluate our spiritual life without also looking at our life in the world. People often find that in seasons of life when they felt accepted by God, they also were accepted by good people. And when God felt unsafe to them, so did the people in their lives. In summary, safety deficits can cut us off from a vital arm of God's resources—his people. And they can also cut us off from closeness with God himself (p. 91).

⟶ *Prayer* ⟵

Father God, that picture of ten-year-old Lynn running, out of control, toward a barbed wire fence but being saved by a strong tree is a powerful illustration of my need for safe people in my life. Thank you for this opportunity to evaluate how many strong trees and how many barbed wire fences are around me. Thank you, too, for showing me some more new things about myself—about how my level of functioning, my physical health, and even my walk with you can all be safety-related. As I go on to work through the rest of this guide, teach me how to break my pattern of heading toward barbed wire and show me how to find more strong trees. Help me trust as I risk getting close to your people and help me to discover a new closeness with you, the God of the Bible, not the God I've imagined due to the barbed wire fences in my life. I pray this in Jesus' name. Amen.

CHAPTER SIX

Why Do I Choose
Unsafe Relationships?

﹍﹏﹍

Roger was disillusioned with relationships. "It seems that every time I make a really close friend, I get screwed," he said, reflecting on his history. "Why can't I find at least one good friend who will not betray me?" Roger was basically asking, "Why do I choose unsafe relationships" (pp. 93–94).

WHY CAN'T I FIND SAFE PEOPLE?

Why don't we see who is safe and who isn't? How is it that some of us seem to have a talent for picking destructive people? Chance doesn't usually cause such a pattern of being hurt in relationships, but rarely do we realize that we are the problem (p. 94).

- Look again at what Jesus says in Matthew 7:1–5. How can our focus on others' faults actually be our own problem in seeing?

Proverbs 4:23 teaches that from our heart flow the issues that we keep finding ourselves caught up in. So if we find that we have recurring dynamics in our lives (such as Jessie's nine marriages to abusive men), we must look first at ourselves to see what in our hearts causes such things to happen. We must look at our own character flaws (p. 95).

- Why is it hard to see what is in our hearts?

- Read the list of character flaws below. What are some possible sources of these flaws that cause us to pick unsafe people?

Inability to Judge Character: *Matters of the heart are mostly subjective and unconscious, but when this emotional side of us and our rational side are in conflict, we are in trouble (pp. 95–96).*

- When have you ignored reason and followed your heart's attraction to a person? What happened?

- Think of patterns in your life. What sort of sickness has your heart been programmed to seek in relationships? (Jessie's heart led her to abusive situations.)

Isolation and Fear of Abandonment: *If we are not able to connect in an intimate way with others, then we will often pick people who are unable to connect as well. The result is isolation, and a fear of abandonment fuels that isolating connection (p. 96).*

- When have you felt more lonely in a relationship than you did outside of that relationship? Are you involved in that sort of isolating relationship today?

- When have you chosen an unsafe relationship rather than no relationship at all? Where are you doing so now?

Defensive Hope: *Humans are incredible optimists when it comes to destructive relationships. But our hope—if we love the hurtful, irresponsible, out of control, abusive, or* *dishonest person correctly or more or enough, that person will change—is a hope that disappoints. We are using hope to defend ourselves against facing the truth about someone we love (p. 97).*

* When has the kind of defensive hope described here kept you in a relationship? What did you realize once that relationship ended?

* Not facing the truth about the person keeps us from having to face grief, sadness, and disappointment. What did you learn from facing the sadness that came when the person in the relationship you mentioned above didn't change and that relationship ended?

Unfaced Badness: *If we do not own our badness, we will—like Joe—often hook up with others for help in keeping alive the illusion that the badness is outside of us, in someone else (pp. 97–98).*

* Think about your relationships. When, if ever, did you hook up with a "loser"? Does this analysis—that you were subconsciously trying to keep alive the illusion that badness is outside of you—fit? Explain.

* What bad parts of yourself have you—in line with the truth of 1 John 1:9–10— come to own and confess? Describe the process. Or, if you're still working on this issue, talk about why you struggle and your plan for doing this important work.

Merger Wishes: *Susie was trying to make up for the things she felt she lacked inside by fusing her identity with Neal. Furthermore, with this strong man by her side, she did not have to learn to formulate goals or be strong (pp. 98–99).*

- Which of your relationships does the description of Neal and Susie remind you of? What feeling about yourself, elements of your past, and/or aspects of your personality motivated your merger wish in that situation?

- What flaws in the other person's character did your merger wishes blind you to? What destructive choices or poor decisions did you make as a result of your merger wishes?

Fear of Confrontation: As Andrea talked about her relationship with her critical friend Sandra, she realized that confronting critical people had always been a problem for her. She found herself unable to talk with that critical, hurtful person, so her pattern continued (pp. 99–100).

- How well do you do when it comes to maintaining good boundaries, confronting others clearly according to biblical guidelines, and resolving problems in relationships? When is it easy? When is it virtually impossible?

- How has your ability to confront served you well—or how has your inability to confront caused you problems and pain?

Romanticizing: This idealized way of looking at a person or a situation omits a big part of reality. In fact, we can turn faults into strengths by viewing them romantically. And, when we romanticize, we can cover up a great deal of disappointment in the past and idealize the future to make up for the sadness we've denied (p. 101).

- When have you, like Chris, romanticized a relationship? Looking back, what faults did you turn into strengths? Be specific.

- Romanticizers do not want reality because it has always disappointed them in their past. How was this the case for you in the relationship you just discussed? What harsh and/or disappointing aspects of reality were you wanting to avoid? What harsh and/or disappointing aspects of reality eventually caught up to you?

Need to Rescue: *As Jerry talked about his relationship with Mindy, he realized that the best times they had were when she needed consoling, or help, or money, or some other crisis intervention by him. They had a rescuing connection rather than a mature interpersonal connection (pp. 101–2).*

- When have you had a rescuing connection with a person? Describe your struggle to end that relationship.

- Explain why rescuing always leads one to unsafe people.

Familiarity: *Tammy seemed addicted to hurtful relationships. As she began to explore this pattern, she saw that all these men were very much like her own father. In those relationships, Tammy was doing what was familiar. She had learned this pattern of relating in her family of origin. It was not something she had to think about. For Tammy and you and me, the familiar just happens—without trying (pp. 102–3).*

- What patterns of relating—both good and bad—did you learn in your family of origin?

- How have you repeated these patterns in your adult relationships? What has resulted from acting on the familiar? And what are you doing to develop new, familiar ways of relating to replace the bad ones that haven't served you well?

Victim Role: A victim is someone who has no power. A victim role, however, is a pattern of relating and behaving of an adult that actually is not powerless anymore, but experiences himself or herself as such and acts out that powerlessness in situations and relationships (pp. 103–4).

• Review the examples of victim language on page 104 of the text. Which phrases remind you of yourself? When have you used such language? When have you chosen—consciously or not—to not take responsibility for your choices and behaviors?

• Explain why victims are prime candidates for unsafe people. What can someone playing a victim role do to change that approach to life and relationships?

Guilt: People who carry guilt often look for someone to play the guilt inducer in their lives, and this guilt inducer often plays the martyr role. The guilty party is hooked into taking responsibility for the other person's pain, anger, or disappointments (pp. 104–5).

• Who has been a guilt inducer in your life? What is the source of guilt within you that gave that person(s) a foothold from which to manipulate you?

• Why can feeling loved by others and understanding our freedom and lack of condemnation in Christ (Rom. 8:1) help free us from guilt and thereby from guilt inducers?

Perfectionism: If people did not see Tom as ideal in whatever context he was in, he was subject to anxiety and would begin to perform to meet the ideal expectations of the person he was with. This perfectionism propelled him toward people who demanded perfection in others, giving Tom an external match for the perfectionist voice in his own head (pp. 105–6).

- Do you have a perfectionist voice in your head? If so, what is its source? How has it impacted your pattern of relationships?

- What can be done to silence that perfectionist voice and free you from the pattern of being drawn to people who demand perfection? Review Tom's situation.

Repetition: *Remember Jessie, the woman who had picked nine unsafe husbands? One reason she did was that she was caught in a destructive relational pattern that she had learned early in life. Sadly, she had never learned anything from her mistakes (pp. 106–7).*

- What destructive relational pattern, if any, did you learn early in life and, having had it "hard-wired" into your brain, have you repeated?

- What did you learn about repetition—and perhaps even about yourself—as you read Jessie's story? What is the way out of a repeated destructive approach to relationships?

Denial of Pain and Perceptions: *We should learn from what we experience over and over (Heb. 5:14), but people whose senses have been dulled do not learn from experience. They do not trust their pain, their perceptions, their feelings, and all the other ways God gave us to discern reality. Consequently, people whose senses have been dulled often get stuck in destructive relationship patterns (pp. 107–8).*

- Where, if at all, do you see yourself in the statement, "They do not trust their pain, their perceptions, their feelings, and all the other ways God gave us to discern reality"? What experiences taught you to deny your pain and perceptions?

- How can safe people, Scripture, a support group, and a therapist help you do what Paul instructs in 1 Thessalonians 5:21–22: "Test everything. Hold on to the good. Avoid every kind of evil"? What source of help are you currently relying on and what are you learning? Or what source will you first turn to—and when?

A NECESSARY PART OF SANCTIFICATION

As you've seen, there are many reasons why we pick unsafe people. It's good for us to look at these reasons, for they are all essential issues of the spiritual life. So look at the list of reasons why we pick unsafe people: an inability to judge character, isolation, defensive hope, unfaced badness, merger wishes, fear of confrontation, romanticizing, rescuing, familiarity, victim roles, guilt, perfectionism, repetition, and denial (p. 108).

- What reasons lie behind your tendency to pick unsafe people? How will dealing with these specific issues contribute to your sanctification process? How does addressing these character flaws—per the Bible's instruction—help you become more like Christ?

- Now explain why finding safe people is necessary to your growth toward spiritual maturity. What role can safe people play in your sanctification? How does God use safe people to help us become spiritually mature?

As you recognize your patterns, you can begin to work on changing them, and you will begin to grow in the grace and knowledge of the Lord. And as you change, the people around you will adapt and change—and you will break the patterns of behavior that have kept you trapped in unsafe relationships. The next chapter will warn you about false solutions you may encounter as you try to change your behavior (pp. 108–9).

— *Prayer* —

Father God, I've come to see more clearly why I choose unsafe relationships. You've helped me realize that an inability to judge character, isolation, defensive hope, unfaced badness, merger wishes, fear of confrontation, romanticizing, rescuing, familiarity, victim roles, guilt, perfectionism, repetition, and denial are among the reasons many of us seem to have a talent for choosing destructive people. More specifically, you've helped me see how I struggle with [list the specific reason(s) you choose unsafe relationships].

Now, Lord, I ask you to show me how to begin the work I need to do to change my patterns. I want to be free of these destructive ways so that I can grow in grace and in my knowledge of you. I pray in the name of Jesus. Amen.

CHAPTER SEVEN

False Solutions

~~

This chapter is designed to save you a lot of time. We'll try to help you see what hasn't worked for you in your relationships—and keep you from wasting time making further mistakes (p. 111).

WHO QUALIFIES?

Everyone has had relational problems. None of us is without cuts or bruises. So, most likely, you'll find some of your unsafe patterns of relating in this chapter. Learn from them. Avoid these potholes, these false solutions that don't work. They don't help you find safe people (p. 111).

- When have you come close to giving up on "this relational thing"? (Maybe you're there now.) What person, event, or situation in your life kept you from giving up? (If you're at this point, let working through this book—especially this chapter—be the event that keeps you from giving up.)

- "Everyone is created to be relational" (Gen. 2:18). What evidence of this truth do you see in the Bible? In your own self?

THE SEVEN "DOINGS"

We'll look at the false solutions as a list of seven "doings." These "doings" are activities and attitudes that seem to promise hope for safe relationships. Yet in reality, they cause conflicts, hurt, and isolation (pp. 111–12).

1. Doing the Same: *The first mistake we make in trying to find safe people is to re-peat history. When we do this, failure and pain aren't teaching us what God intended them to (Prov. 26:11) (pp. 112–13).*

- What did you learn from Rob and Lu Ann?

- Sit back in an armchair with a cup of coffee and reflect on your most recent rela-tional failure. Ask yourself, "Why didn't that relationship work out?"

- What pattern(s) have you repeated in your relational history? Let this specific, black-and-white list help you learn from your past and avoid "doing the same" in the future.

2. Doing the Opposite: *It's easy to knee jerk when you've been hurt, so we often make extreme moves based on our pain and confusion. We don't solve our relational problems this way; we just switch them (pp. 113–15).*

- What, if anything, do you see of yourself in Toby's wanderings?

- Look again at the list of opposites on pages 114 and 115 of the text. Which reac-tive pattern of falling in love have you fallen into? Which friends are opposite from your family of origin? When have you reactively chosen religious settings?

- When we split, we see one type of relationship as all-good and another as all-bad. Think about a relationship in your life that you labeled "all-bad." What good and godly qualities were in the person and relationship that you would do well to look for in another person and relationship?

- People are more than the sum total of their unsafe traits. But, in an effort to learn from your past and develop good judgment (Ps. 119:66), list hurtful traits of unsafe people you've had contact with. Let this list help you filter out, discern, and evaluate the character of people in your life today so that you can avoid "doing the opposite."

3. Doing Too Much: We need to actively seek relationship with God and others, and many people have found healthy friendships on the way to learning waltz steps or golf swings. But many people stay in such functional arenas because they are afraid of relationship. Having a project to work on and talk about provides the semblance of relationship, but without risk (pp. 115–17).

- When has your life been filled with activities the way Linda's was? In terms of developing relationships, what resulted from your busyness?

- List your current activities. In each, are relationships more accidental than purposeful? Asked differently, which activity(ies) have the stated purpose of helping people get connected?

- Task completion is good, but closeness to God and others must always take precedence (Luke 10:42). So plan your busyness carefully. Where will you go to find groups and activities designed and intended for fostering closeness? What is the first step you'll take—and when will you take it?

4. Doing Nothing: *Doing nothing is not the way to get plugged into a place where you can be connected to good relationships (Heb. 10:38) (pp. 117–19).*

- Review the examples of the "doing nothing" approach listed on page 118 of the text. Which of these strategies have you adopted in the past? Which are you following today?

- Do you struggle when it comes to taking initiative? That's the case for many "nothing doers." If so, try to figure out why. Were you ever abandoned or punished for taking initiative? Or were you taught to be passive (see p. 119)?

- What will you do about your "do nothing" tendency and the root causes of it? When will you take the first step?

5. Doing for Others: *The idea here is that, in serving, we are blessed; in giving, we receive; and in helping, we are assisted. Properly understood, this is a biblical principle (Isa. 58:10), but the problem with applying it to finding safe people is our motive. God wants us to give, serve, and help—but not out of emptiness, loneliness, or a need to be loved (1 Cor. 13:3). When giving protects us, it has turned to selfishness (pp. 119–20).*

- When have you used "doing for others" as a false solution for finding safe people and relationships? What resulted?

- Many of us do for others in an attempt to find safety and in order to avoid our loneliness, our inability to ask people for comfort, our helplessness, or our feelings of being "one-down." Which of these needs have you avoided through helping others?

- It's humbling—and difficult and threatening—to ask for what we need. Talk about a time when you have gotten up the nerve to ask for what you needed. How did the (hopefully safe) person you asked respond? What did you learn from that experience?

- What current needs do you have? Whom could you ask for help or comfort, company or counsel? Ask God to help you first ask to receive and then help you receive what his people have to give you.

6. Doing "Cosmetic Personality Surgery": *Another futile yet very common approach to finding safe people is making external changes in ourselves that aren't true heart changes. These attempts can give us false hope and then disappoint us greatly (pp. 120–21).*

- Look again at the examples of cosmetic personality surgery (p. 121 of the text). Which have you attempted in an effort to become more relational? What resulted from those attempts?

- Fear of intimacy, not an intro line, was what Keith needed help with. What did (or do) you need help with that cosmetic personality surgery does not address?

What will you do to begin that hard but important work to become the unique person God intends you to be (Eph. 4:16)?

7. *Doing Without:* *Doing without is the final resting place for many who have tried the preceding six false solutions. It is where people go who have given up hoping for relationship. It is a quiet place of despair (Prov. 13:12) (p. 122).*

• Doing without is also a place of harsh judgment (see the list on p. 122). Which conclusions about yourself have you come to?

• Are you still feeling the pain of isolation—or has that disconnected part of your soul withered away? Take heart. Know that reading this book is a positive step that indicates that part of you is still alive—and keep reading.

Because this last false solution—doing without—is so prevalent and so hurtful, we will spend more time on it in the following chapter as we examine why we often choose to isolate ourselves from relationships. Right now may you find comfort in the fact that God hurts for you in your aloneness. He feels what you are going through and he wants to remove you from these false solutions and set you on a new path (p. 122).

⟶ *Prayer* ⟵

Father God, you've shown me the false paths I've been on in my search for safe and nurturing relationships. You've helped me realize that many of my cuts and bruises from the relational arena come from doing the same, doing the opposite, doing too much, doing nothing, doing for others, and/or doing cosmetic personality surgery. And you know, perhaps better than I, how close I am to doing without to the point of having part of my soul wither away like a starving infant. You know the pain of my aloneness. So I come to you for comfort and hope. I also ask you, God, to make known to me "the path of life" [Prov. 15:24]. May I sense your presence by my side as I seek to trust that the path you show me is a path of safety. I pray in Jesus' name. Amen.

Chapter Eight

Why Do I Isolate Myself from People?

Like Ted, many people—and perhaps you're one of them—have tried again and again to connect with safe people, only to find pain and failure. And now you've simply given up. You've stopped the attempt and the search. It's just not worth it anymore. This chapter explains the dynamics of such withdrawal and isolation. We'll help you understand the most important reasons you might have given up the fight to find the right kinds of friends, churches, and loved ones—and we'll help you see biblical solutions (p. 124).

A BROKEN HEART

Our hearts aren't all that strong. God has constructed us with certain needs and certain limitations. Our most basic and primary need is to be loved by God and people. When our need to take in sustenance from other people is thwarted, we are injured. Our hearts start to break down when we do not receive love.

In the story that opens this chapter, Ted suffered from a broken heart and was able, after some hard work on his part, to point to the specific time he gave up on being loved (p. 124).

- What causes of your broken heart are you aware of? What people, situations, and events have caused you to lose the ability to trust, to need, and to reach out for attachment?

You may be better able to answer the previous question by looking at three reasons why people lose the ability to trust—abandonment, inconsistent attachment, and attack (p. 125).

Abandonment: *Like Ted, some people are left emotionally by a significant person—a parent, spouse, or friend. When this happens, we lose our sense of expectation of love, and eventually we lose our sense of need (Ps. 69:20) (p. 125).*

- Who, if anyone, has abandoned you? When did that happen?

Inconsistent Attachment: *Being loved in an unpredictable manner can also cause brokenheartedness. The person in relationship with an inconsistent person is always waiting for the other shoe to drop. He or she always worries that the love given will be snatched away. That kind of love is very different from the love of God (John 10:29) (pp. 125–26).*

- Who in your life has been an emotional roller coaster for you? Whose love was unpredictable and unreliable, one time being there and close, the next time enraged or not there at all?

Attack: *Love doesn't exist outside of risk, but there are those who deliberately hurt the hurting (Ps. 109:16). If your need for love has been attacked, you probably learned very quickly how to shun relationship and find other ways to pass the time (p. 126).*

- Who, if anyone, in your life has criticized or even abused you for having the need for love?

Remember that, if you qualify as brokenhearted in any or all of these three categories—in your past or in the present—God "heals the brokenhearted and binds up [your] wounds" (Ps. 147:3). Know, too, that safe people are out there—and in Part 3 we'll describe them and how to find them (p. 126).

- Did you, like Ted, ever make a conscious decision to stop needing people? If so, when?

- How well is your isolation working for you?

SELF-SUFFICIENCY

Three-year-old Benny is in love with autonomy, task mastery, and individuation. This functional self-sufficiency is very different from the relational self-sufficiency that many hurting people strive for (pp. 126–27).

- What elements of the emotional philosophy of relational self-sufficiency (see p. 127) have you bought into? Which characterize your approach to life today?

- God doesn't create us to be relationally self-sufficient. He wants us to need each other, for our needs teach us about love and keep us humble. Despite the fact that true self-sufficiency is a product of the Fall, which of the advantages of self-sufficiency do you enjoy? See the list on page 128.

Giving up self-sufficiency is a difficult process. The first step is to confess, or tell the truth about, your need for people. As you confess to safe people your problem with self-sufficiency, a wonderful miracle happens over time. Your self-sufficiency melts and gives way to need. You can then be reconciled not only to God and others, but also to yourself (p. 128).

- Who in your life understands self-sufficiency and its pitfalls? Which of these people will you talk with?

- When you meet with this person, what will you say about why you are disconnected? What will you say to explain how hard it is to give up your indepen-
  dence? Practice now.

AN INABILITY TO EXPERIENCE HUNGER

*In the spiritual and relational arena, some people literally cannot feel their hunger
for relationships. Often unaware of their need and numb to their emptiness, they starve
themselves when they should be connecting with others (pp. 128–29).*

- Which, if any, of the classic hallmarks of spiritual anorexia do you have? See the
  list on page 129.

- If, for you, relationship is an unneeded option rather than a God-given hunger designed to tell us to get connected, what will you do to start experiencing your
  need for relationship? After all, God wants to waken that sleeping part of you; he
  wants you to hunger and thirst for righteous and loving people (Matt. 5:6).

DEVALUATION

*Devaluation is the "sour grapes" mentality: "Those grapes I wanted probably weren't
any good anyway." Translated, this means, "I really wanted those grapes. Since I can't
have them, it hurts inside, and I don't like that sort of pain. Making the grapes bad makes
me hurt less." Devaluation is making ourselves not want what we don't have. But need
is a good part of you. Even God himself experiences longings, as Christ did when he
mourned over his unrepentant people (Matt. 23:37). Devaluing the person who hurt you
rather than letting yourself miss the good parts of that person, and still hating the bad
parts that hurt you, can indeed seem like the easy way to cope with relational hurts (pp.
130–31).*

- When have you, like Peter, devalued the person who hurt you?

- Review the list of traits on pages 130–31. Where, if at all, do you see yourself in this description of a person who tends toward devaluation?

- When have you, like Alison, let yourself grieve and finally reach the point of ambivalence, having both good and bad feelings toward the one who hurt you? Why is this approach—which is often more difficult—to the end of a relationship a healthier one?

- If, despite your new understanding of the drawbacks of devaluing, you know you tend to be a devaluer, what will you do to help yourself get over that pattern? Choose from the list of steps on pages 131–32 of the text and be specific as to how and when you will take that step.

PERFECTIONISM

Perfectionism is an inability to tolerate faults. Perfectionists have a phobia about imperfections and blemishes in themselves, in other people, and in the world. The perfectionist runs in futility from the realities of sin, age, loss, and cellulite and tries to live in the land of ideals where fairness and equality should rule. On a deeper level, the perfectionist lives under the Law: "If you do it right, you'll be loved."

Perfectionism cuts us off from safe relationships by disqualifying us from connection. The impossible standard of who we "should" be constantly reminds us of our failings, sins, and weaknesses. Perfectionism also disqualifies others from connection, focusing us on what needs to be fixed in a person and blinding us to the lovable parts (pp. 132–33).

- How, if at all, has perfectionism cut you off from safe relationships? Have you disqualified yourself or other people? Be specific.

- Where do you see yourself in the description of perfectionists as critical of others, projecting a deep self-hatred on others, and feeling the need to be treated specially? Look also at the list of qualities on page 134 of the text.

- If you have recognized that you are a perfectionist, what will you do to get free of that approach to life and relationships and self? Choose from the list of steps on page 134 of the text and be specific as to how and when you will take that step.

MERGER WISHES

A merger wish is basically love minus boundaries. When someone else possesses a trait that we don't have, we are inclined to blur our identity with theirs in order to help us feel better about ourselves and to gain access to that trait. Merging also keeps us from feeling alone.

People who struggle with merger wishes are sometimes terrified and discouraged by the realities of separateness. Separateness feels like total abandonment, not freedom. So the "merging" person concludes, "It's better to be without a relationship than to risk the reality of feeling separate" (pp. 134–36).

- Do you see yourself in Vicky's thought process as she tried to call Rick? Explain your answer.

- How do you feel about separateness when you encounter it in a relationship? How do you deal with the reality of separateness?

- If you've given up on relationship because you've been disappointed and felt abandoned too many times, you need to take some steps to get back on the road to choosing connections. Look at the list on pages 136–37. Which step will you take? How and when will you take that step? Be specific.

PASSIVITY

To be passive is to avoid action. God never reinforces passivity. He always presents our growth as a partnership with him. He does what only God can do, and we do our job: "work out [our] salvation with fear and trembling" (Phil. 2:12). To avoid responsibility is never a spiritual act. Kevin was one of the most laid-back guys around, and as a result he finally lost everything and everyone he loved. And Kevin is like a lot of people, although perhaps more severe than most (pp. 137–38).

- Do you tend toward passivity? In what situations are you most passive? What has your passivity cost you in terms of family, relationships, and career?

- What may be behind your passivity? Some possibilities are listed on pages 137–38 of the text.

- For what are you waiting now? Are you waiting for God to help you find a job or a mate, solve a relational problem, find a support group, or heal emotional pain—without you doing anything toward that specific end? Are you waiting for the phone to ring, someone at work to befriend you, or a church member to greet you?

- At times, waiting can be exactly the right thing to do. But remember that, throughout life, you need to do your part too, for "if he shrinks back, I will not be pleased with him" (Heb. 10:38). What will you do to find people who want to help you enter the world, encourage you to take action, and support your attempts to regain control over your life and relationships?

Odds are, in these last two chapters, you've seen yourself in a few areas. There are specific reasons you choose to get into unsafe relationships. There are also reasons you avoid developing relationships at all. Now that you've understood the problem, it's time to look at the solution. In part 3, you'll come to understand what safe people are, why we need them, where to find them, and—most important of all—how to become a safe person yourself (pp. 138–39).

— *Prayer* —

Father God, you know when and how my heart has been broken. Like no one else, you know the pain I've felt and still feel. You know how I lost the ability to trust—the abandonment, the inconsistent attachment, the attacks—and my fear of learning to trust again. And, God, I'm trying to know you as One who heals the brokenhearted and binds up our wounds, and that could be a big job for me.

     Lord, you know why I've tried to hide behind the facade of self-sufficiency or come to the point of being unable to experience any hunger for relationships. You know my tendency to devalue people who hurt me, my perfectionism that disqualifies me and/or others from relationships, my merger wishes that make it hard to tolerate separateness, and my passivity. Through this study, you've shown me why I choose unsafe relationships, and you've encouraged me to take some steps to break those patterns. Help me not be content with merely a new level of self-understanding. Again I ask, Lord, that you will give me the courage and perseverance to take the necessary steps toward safe relationships, toward people who can help me become the person you intend me to be. I pray in the name of my Lord and Savior Jesus Christ. Amen.

PART THREE

Safe People

CHAPTER NINE

What Are Safe People?

———

When I (John) had breakfast with Mark, I acted as a safe person for Mark to confide in. Just as surely as we were taking in our breakfast to sustain us physically, so we were talking to sustain ourselves emotionally. We were enjoying the great benefits of a safe relationship (p. 143).

WHAT IS A SAFE RELATIONSHIP?

A safe relationship draws us closer to God, draws us closer to others, and helps us become the real person God created us to be. When we are in a safe relationship, we fulfill the greatest commandment, to love God (Matt. 22:37–38); we keep the second commandment, to love each other (Matt. 22:39); and we grow into the particular person God created us to be, accomplishing the tasks he has designed for us (Eph. 2:10) (pp. 143–44).

• Who in your life comes to mind as you read this definition of a safe relationship? Thank God for that person—and for the fact that you've at least brushed shoulders with a safe person even though it may feel as if you know only unsafe people.

• Read the descriptions of a safe person listed on page 144 of the text. This more conversational definition of a safe person may bring to mind the names of other safe people you've known. What other safe people have either crossed your path or, ideally, taken up residency in your life?

Before we address the problem of how to recognize safe people, we need to first understand what a safe person is and why we need that kind of safety. The best example of a safe person is found in Jesus. In him were found the three qualities of a safe person: dwelling, grace, and truth (John 1:14) (p. 145).

Dwelling: *Dwelling refers to someone's ability to connect with us. The Greek behind this New Testament word means "encamp" or "reside" and has to do with the human body as the place where the spirit encamps. What this means is that safe relationships are an aspect of the incarnational qualities of Jesus (p. 145).*

- Who in your life has been a flesh-and-bones Jesus for you? Describe the situation. What did that person do and say to let you know that he or she was very present with you?

- Perhaps your hurts and resultant fears have kept you from getting close enough to anyone to experience God's presence through a human being. How would you benefit if you were to find someone who could be present with you in the joy and pain of life?

- What do you do and say to let someone you're with know that you are present with him or her?

Grace: *Grace is "unmerited favor." Grace implies unconditional love and acceptance with no condemnation (Rom. 8:1; Eph. 4:32). Grace says that you are accepted just as you are and that you will not be shamed or incur wrath for whatever you are experiencing (p. 145).*

- Who has offered you a taste of God's grace by accepting you unconditionally and without condemnation?

- Perhaps you haven't ever let yourself really be known by another person. What benefits do you think you would receive if you were to find unconditional love and acceptance in a relationship? Do you see those benefits outweighing the risk? (Take the risk only after you've worked through the section on recognizing safe people!)

- To whom in your life can you offer unconditional love and acceptance? When will you start?

Truth: *In relationships, truth implies being honest and real with one another, and living out the truth of God. Safe relationships don't give grace alone; they give grace and confrontation. And we all need friends who walk according to the truth, who live out the principles of God with us, and who, in their acceptance of us, are honest about our faults without condemning us (Gal. 6:1) (p. 146).*

- Who has offered you truth as well as grace? Who has been honest about your faults without condemning you, thereby helping you become the person God intends you to be? What did you learn about yourself from that experience? And what did you learn about safe relationships?

- Perhaps in your efforts to be loved and accepted, you've never let anyone get close enough to see, much less talk about, your faults. If you were to let a safe person close, how would you benefit from that person's ability to speak the truth in love about your sins and shortcomings?

- In the past, you may have been short on grace when you've confronted people about something. To whom should you apologize? Do so. Now plan how you will speak the truth with love—how you will extend grace as you confront—the next time you need to be honest about someone's faults.

In the rest of this book, we will be examining different aspects of dwelling, grace, and truth. The calling of the Bible is that we need to be the kind of people to each other that Jesus is with us, people who dwell with each other in grace and truth (p. 146).

— Prayer —

Father God, I have so many reasons to thank you for your Son. Now I see that he can teach me much about safe people since he is the ultimate model of a safe person. Thank you for the dwelling, the grace, and the truth he offers me. Thank you that he knows what I'm feeling and can sympathize with my struggles and pain (Heb. 4:15). Thank you that Jesus offers me the supreme grace of unconditional love and acceptance, that you and he accept me just as I am and without causing me shame or making me a target of wrath because of what I'm experiencing. And thank you that the truth that Jesus embodies is a truth that helps me become the person you want me to be. It's not a truth that avoids confrontation and lets me stay stuck in my sinful, faulty ways. I now look forward to learning how I can offer dwelling, grace, and truth to other people and how I can learn to identify those safe people—your people— who will offer those things to me. Continue to teach me, heal me, and encourage me. I pray in Jesus' name. Amen.

CHAPTER TEN

Why Do We Need Safe People?

⌒⌒

When he was a young boy, the pastor we worked with said to himself, "I will never trust anyone again"—and he lived out that promise. Doing so took its toll on him through the years. Having hundreds of people that he ministered to and was around all the time did not fill the void inside that the wall had created. Jesus shows us how to break down walls like that. Again and again, he and his followers taught that good human relationships are one of the primary ways that God changes our lives and heals us (1 Peter 4:10) (p. 147).

THE CHURCH

Too often, people don't think of turning to the body of Christ as God's agent and answer to their prayers when they're hurting. But God does not separate our relationship with God from our relationship with people in his body. In fact, the Bible says that if we do not have good, loving relationships with people, we do not know God either (1 John 4:20). What many Christians do not understand is that relating to each other is a spiritual activity. The Bible teaches clearly that we need others in order to grow into the people that God wants us to be (pp. 147–48).

- When has relating to a brother or sister in the Lord actually seemed like a spiritual activity? Asked differently, when has a good, loving relationship with one of God's people helped you come to know God a little better?

- Spirituality is a life of love both with God and with each other (Matt. 22:40). So, to evaluate your spiritual life, ask yourself, "How am I doing with other people? How are my relationships going?" What do your relationships indicate about your spiritual growth?

FUEL

We are actually supplied with what we need from others in the body of Christ (Col. 2:19). Good old-fashioned support is the basic fuel we need to face and deal with the trials and discouragements of life.

As a result of many hurts in her early relationships, Jane began to feel worthless and unlovable whenever she faced conflict or when someone didn't approve of her. She withdrew from almost everyone and, in this withdrawal, became more and more tired and less motivated (pp. 148–49).

- When have you experienced a tiredness caused by disconnection and isolation from other people? Describe the circumstances.

- In sharp contrast, when have you found new energy and enthusiasm for life in relationship?

- Where is your energy level today? What might that be saying about your current level of connectedness or isolation? What will you do with what you've just realized about yourself?

COMFORT

When Paul was depressed and discouraged, God comforted him by sending him a friend in Titus (2 Cor. 7:6). People who are grieving will tell you that a combination of God's presence and the support of other people gave them the comfort they needed. After all, comfort is one thing we are not made to give ourselves.

Penelope said, "I thought I would never get over the death of my husband. . . . The only way that I made it through was because of my friends who would sit with me while I despaired. It was not what they said that helped; it was the fact that they were there" (pp. 149–50).

- When in your grief have you realized that God's presence is not enough? Or, asked differently, when in your grief have you experienced God's comfort through one of his people?

- When has the fact that someone was there with you been a source of comfort? Describe the situation (you may use the one you just referred to) and what the person did and said, if anything.

- For whom could you be a comforting presence today? Remember that you don't need words; you just need to be there.

FOR STRENGTH IN SETTING BOUNDARIES

One of our greatest needs for emotional and spiritual health is to have healthy boundaries. We need to have the ability to say no to evil, and sometimes this evil comes from hurtful people. Sadly, we sometimes don't have the strength to stand up to it on our own.

Mary tried to be loving to everyone in her life, but whenever a relationship required her to be strong and confront someone sinning against her (Matt. 18:15), Mary was un-

able to do it—until she found support in a group for spouses of problem drinkers (p. 150).

- When have you found in other people strength for "hands that are weak and knees that are feeble" so that you could "be healed" (Heb. 12:12–13 NASB)? Be specific about how people have helped you find the strength you need to set and keep boundaries.

- What boundaries do you especially struggle to set and maintain? Who in your life helps you do that—or where will you go to find someone to help you?

- For whom are you (or could you be) a source of strength in setting boundaries? What are you doing to offer support?

FOUNDATION FOR AGGRESSION

Often we think of aggression as something negative. But aggression can be good, helping us achieve our purpose in life. Passive people, however, do not know how to use their God-given aggression to go out and attack life and accomplish the goals God has set before them.

Raised by a passive father and a domineering mother, Patrick was a passive man. Many of his dreams went unfulfilled and responsibilities unmet. When Patrick finally got into a good, safe support group, he received from the strong men in it the modeling his father never gave him. He saw how to become the strong man his wife needed him to be (p. 151).

- Do you tend to be passive when it comes to tackling life and pursuing goals? If so, where will you go to find the role models you need?

- Perhaps you used to be more passive than you are today. Who in your life modeled strength and healthy aggression?

- While you were growing up, your parents may have modeled a healthily aggressive approach to life. What didn't your original family provide for you? How might good relationships in the family of God give you those things?

ENCOURAGEMENT AND SUPPORT

"Fighting the good fight" is discouraging, and we often need direct encouragement from God and his Word (Rom. 15:4; Phil. 2:1). But the Bible also emphatically says that we need to be encouraged by each other (Eph. 6:21–22). Even the apostle Paul, whom we often consider a spiritual giant, writes in many places that the encouragement and love of others kept him going through difficult times (pp. 151–52).

- Look again at the images of Ecclesiastes 4:9–12. When has someone helped you up after you have fallen down? When have God's people come alongside you so that you wouldn't be overpowered? Be specific.

- Who is a primary encourager in your life? How does he or she do that? And how does that person know when you need encouragement? Think about what receiving encouragement requires from the one doing the receiving!

- Whom can and will you encourage today—and how? Maybe your encourager needs some encouragement in the form of a thank you!

MODELING

Many people come from families that did not teach and model God's ways (Deut. 6:7; Prov. 22:6). All of us are lacking in those areas of life where we have not received the modeling we needed. These could be strength or boundaries (as we have seen) as well as compassion, empathy, love, marriage, career development, fun, talents and skills, relationship skills, forgiveness, and sex-role development. In fact, all of us are members of Adam's dysfunctional family, and we need more than help. We need to be "born again" and become like children. We need to learn to live in his family with him as our Father (p. 152).

• In what areas of life did you not receive the modeling you needed?

• Who in the body of Christ has parented, taught, and mentored you—or where will you go to find someone who will?

• For whom have you been able to model something about how to live in God's family? Whether that role is one you are playing now or one you will play sometime in the future, explain how members of God's family can pass on generational health.

HEALING

One of the major factors in the healing of any emotional disorder is grief. We need to grieve painful events, painful losses, love that will never be realized, dreams that have been crushed, and many other hurts that life inflicts upon us (Matt. 16:25). When we do mourn, we find comfort (Matt. 5:4). But we can't grieve what we need to grieve without something new to attach to, and that's why grieving takes relationship.

We must have God and others to connect to in order to let go of what we have lost. As Paul told the Corinthians, if they would connect to him, they could let go of their other "affections" (emotional ties) that were restraining them (2 Cor. 6:11–13 NASB) (pp. 152–53).

- What hurts and losses have you needed to grieve in the past? What hurts and losses do you still need to grieve?

- If you've done some grieving, to whom did you "open wide," thereby gaining support and the new ground you needed to stand on as you let go of what you were grieving? Describe the process you went through and the results.

- If you know you need to grieve and let go, where will you go to find support? Also, if you are familiar with the grieving process, whom—if anyone—can you walk alongside and provide support?

CONFRONTATION AND DISCIPLINE

The areas that we usually most need to change, we are unaware of; we know, but resist owning; or we know and openly rebel against. We need our brothers and sisters to make us aware of our behavior, confront our denial, and take a stand against our rebellion. "Safe people" in our lives confront and discipline us when we need it, and they do so with a spirit of grace and truth (Gal. 6:1). When such confrontation doesn't get our attention and motivate us to change, intervention is the next step (Matt. 18:15–18).

It was painful but helpful for staff members to help me (Henry) become aware of times that I had not listened to their feelings but been quick with an argument. They helped me see the truth that I needed to change a pattern of relating (pp. 153–55).

- When has someone confronted you about a certain behavior or sin in your life? How did they communicate a spirit of grace and truth? How did you respond initially? What did you learn about yourself from the incident? What did you do as a result of the confrontation? How, in the long run, have you benefited from the confrontation?

- Perhaps you've been confronted and have dismissed the incident. Why were you defensive and deaf to the point being made? What does the Bible say about someone who will not heed the discipline of others? (See Prov. 12:5; 15:5; 17:10.) Think through that incident and see whether there is in fact something to be gained from what was said to you.

- When have you boldly loved someone and confronted him or her about a hurtful pattern of living? What happened as a result of your tough love? If you haven't ever confronted someone, what do you now recognize about the kind of love you may be offering your friends?

GOOD DEEDS

The Bible tells us that we need to be stimulated by each other to do good things. Our relationships help us be encouraged to lives of service (Heb. 10:24–25). We need to be around those believers who help us to grow and become the people God made us to be.

The two high school students were always "good kids," but a missions trip pushed them into a new dimension of life that is better than any: service to others. When they went with other believers and saw service in action and what it could do, their lives were changed (p. 155).

- When have others spurred you on "toward love and good deeds" (Heb. 10:24–25) as the mission team did for the high-schoolers? Talk about the experience and your reaction to what you saw about the value of service to others.

- Where is God calling you to serve? How is he using his people to encourage you to serve him?

- How might God want to use you to spur people on "toward love and good deeds," toward service to him and his people? Whose gifts might you affirm? Whose service might you encourage?

ROOTING AND GROUNDING

The Bible refers to the body of Christ as being "knit together" in love (Col. 2:2 NASB), and this fact helps give us the support we need in order to grow and go through the trials of life. We need to be grounded in the body of Christ to find the strength we need. When we let ourselves be rooted and grounded in God's unified and therefore strong body, we will be able to weather the storms of life (Matt. 7:24–25).

Even when all the structures that had given Dennis a sense of what day-to-day life was about were suddenly gone, he knew that he still had God and his friends to depend on and that, in those relationships, he would be able to find the grounding and stability that he was going to need to put his life back together. Dennis knew people who formed a safe unit for him, just as the disciples did for one another (John 17:11, 22) (pp. 155–57).

- When has your life crumbled around you? Where did you turn for support and stability? If you looked to God's family, what did you find there?

- What storms of life are God's family helping you weather today? Describe what you are receiving from them and the forms their support is taking.

- Whom are you—or could you be—supporting as the storms of life rage around him or her? What are you—or could you be—doing to be a vessel of God's strength, hope, and encouragement?

<u>LOVE</u>

In relationships we learn to love. When we receive love, this teaches us how to love (1 John 4:19). Jesus himself teaches us to love others as he loved us (John 13:34). Loving people are loving because they have been loved and have followed that example. And, as we have seen, one of the important ways God loves us and thereby teaches us to love is through the body of believers.

As we place ourselves in good, loving relationships and as we receive and respond to that love, we learn how God wants us to love others, and we can go and do likewise. Also, I know I would never have grown in the way I needed to if I had not been involved closely enough with people to get tested. If we never have close relationships, we can be under the delusion that we really are loving (pp. 157–58).

- What lessons about love—how to be loving, how to receive love—have you learned in good relationships? How have those lessons inspired and empowered you to be a more loving person?

- In close relationships, we also learn the ways in which we fail to love correctly. What have you learned from people about how unloving you can be? How did their confrontation and forgiveness help you change your ways?

- In what relationship(s) are you modeling the kind of love God wants us to have for one another? In general, what lessons about love (good and perhaps bad) are you teaching (consciously or not) those people with whom you are in relationship?

Safety is as safety does. And safety is dwelling, grace, and truth. We all need this kind of safety from other people. God designed us for safe people, and in the context of his family of safe people, we can grow into the image of his Son, who was and is the ultimate Safe Person (p. 158).

— *Prayer* —

Father God, I really do need safe people in my life. I see more clearly than ever how other believers are indeed your instruments of grace [1 Peter 4:10], and that helps me be more open to taking the risks involved in new relationships. And so do the possible rewards—fuel for life, comfort when I'm low, strength in setting and maintaining boundaries, a foundation for healthy aggression, encouragement and support for "fighting the good fight," modeling in those areas of life where my original family didn't show me your ways, healing and the chance to grieve, confrontation and discipline when I'm either unaware of, denying, or rebelling against my need to change, encouragement toward good deeds and a life of service, and rooting and grounding when life falls apart.

Thank you for this marvelous plan—that you meet us where we are, love us, heal us, free us, and teach us through your people. Building relationships with "safe people" is now sounding more like a wonderful adventure in faith than a task I must, with gritted teeth, do for my own good. Thank you for renewed hope and a spark of excitement—and thank you that you'll be with me as I look for safe people and learn myself how to be safe. I pray in Jesus' name. Amen.

CHAPTER ELEVEN

Where Are the Safe People?

Perhaps you've discovered a real and difficult truth: the church is not a totally safe place, and it doesn't consist of only safe people. As much as we would like for it to be totally safe, the truth is that the church has to be seen the way God describes it. Our faith must be able to square with the reality of life as we find it and _with the reality that the Bible describes to us. Let's look at these two realities (p. 160)._

REALITY AS PEOPLE FIND IT

Like Theresa, anyone who has been in the church for long has been hurt by people in the church. For even in the body of Christ, we find some harsh realities: judgment, pride, self-centeredness, manipulation, abandonment, abuse, control, perfectionism, domination, and every kind of relational sin known to humankind. The walls of the church do not make it safe from sin. In fact, the church by definition is composed of sinners (1 Tim. 1:15) (p. 160).

• What hurts have you experienced from people in the church? What sins have you been disappointed to find even in God's church?

• As the family of God, the church activates our most primitive and dependent longings. What longings for security, love, and a perfect family did you take into the church? Which of those have been crushed?

The church is both safe and dangerous. Sometimes we are fortunate to find good relationships, and other times we run into disaster. So take a moment now to consider the positive aspects of the reality of the church (p. 162).

- When have you felt nurtured and loved in the body of Christ? Be specific.

- What freeing truths have you learned? What healing have you experienced in the family of God (Eph. 4:16; 1 Peter 4:10)?

REALITY AS THE BIBLE DESCRIBES IT

Sadly, our ideals for the church do not reflect biblical reality any more than they match the reality we experience. While we may think that the Bible promises a church where we find only safe people, God's Word actually teaches that the church is full of wolves as well as sheep. If we are going to find healing and minimize the hurt we can find in church, we need to make sure we see the church as God describes it. We need to operate according to biblical reality instead of our fantasized wishes, for biblical reality is the one that will fit the experience we find in the real world (p. 162).

- Look again at the story Jesus tells in Matthew 13:24–30. What does this story teach about whom you will find in the church?

- Now look at the parable of the sower Jesus tells in Matthew 13:18–23. What does this story teach about the kind of destructive, hurtful people you will find in God's church?

- What is God saying to you through Jesus' parable of the sower? What kind of person are you in his church?

WISDOM AND CHARACTER

Our experience and the Bible both affirm that the church is full of safe people, unsafe people, and hurtful lingerers. There is no perfect family this side of heaven, but neither is there an absolute hell full of only demons. That's why we must be discerning. We must be careful, make informed choices, and, rather than becoming pessimistic and skeptical, learn to recognize the goodness that abounds within God's family (Matt. 25:34–40). The long and short of it is that we have to work to find safe people. We have to use our wisdom, discernment, and character. And we gain wisdom and discernment through knowledge and experience (p. 164).

- What knowledge gained through this study will help you in your efforts to discern safe people? Give two or three examples of helpful points you've learned.

- What wisdom and ability to discern have you gained through your experience in both hurtful and good relationships, with unsafe people as well as safe people? Refer to the learning experiences as well as the lessons learned.

- If our own character problems (the type we've looked at in earlier chapters) get in the way of using our knowledge and experience, we will make poor choices. What weaknesses inside (character problems) are you now facing and ready to deal with?

SOME OPTIONS

Within the body of Christ, God has gifted people to heal each other. We have found these people in a variety of settings and structures, from informal to formal. We'll look at four of them (p. 164).

__Safe Churches:__ One place to find safe people is in churches that, as a group, have a safe character. You need a church that not only has good orthodox doctrine but is also a body where relationship is preached and community is formed (pp. 164–65).

- Think of unsafe churches you've attended. Which of the qualities of safe churches (listed on p. 165 of the text) do you now see were absent?

- How does the church you currently attend look when you see it through the lens of these questions? And what does this evaluation tell you about that church? Or, if you aren't attending a church, what concrete things will you look for as a result of reading this list?

__Restorative Friendships:__ We believe that friendship is the most powerful tool God uses to change and heal character. In relationships with others we are healed, our character is changed, and sanctification happens (p. 165).

- When has a friend's support and prayer had the kind of healing impact that Louise's friend had on her? What healing did God give you through that friendship?

- Good, safe friends give us what we need in the areas of acceptance, support, discipline, modeling, and a host of other relationship ingredients that produce change. Which of these elements were present in the friendship you referred to above? Which are present in a current friendship and what impact is that friendship having on your life, your character, and your spiritual growth?

- Look again at the list of qualities crucial to a good friendship that produces growth (pp. 166–67 of the text). What does this list show you about friendships that have gone bad? About some of your current friendships? And about the kind of friend God calls you to be?

Support Groups: *Groups are an extremely powerful tool for spiritual and emotional growth. While we, or one other person, may not be able to stand up to our character problems, a group is stronger (Eccl. 4:12). Furthermore, a dynamic occurs in a group that is absent in one-on-one relationships: members realize the universality of pain and suffering, and they are not as tempted to condemn themselves (p. 167).*

- When, if ever, have you experienced this dynamic? Comment on your reaction. If you've never been in a group, share your thoughts about why this dynamic can be so healing for many people.

- For what character problems or past hurts might a group be helpful? How can a group, existing for the expressed purpose of helping people with the exact issue(s) you just identified, also help the hurting person learn to trust?

- Explain the value of having a group that is structured, has an expressed purpose, and has experienced leadership. Where will you go to find such a group? Whom will you ask for references and leads?

Individual Therapy: *Individual therapy is a powerful, proven method of dealing with deep issues and developmental impasses (p. 168).*

*   When have you experienced some of the benefits of individual therapy? What were some of the things you gained from therapy?

*   If you've considered therapy but never tried it, what would you hope to gain from specialized one-on-one attention with an expert in your area of need?

*   Explain the importance of checking out a therapist's credentials and talking to people who know his or her work. Where will you go to find a skilled therapist? Whom will you ask for references and leads?

There are many safe people in God's church. As you look for them, however, make sure you use discernment, wisdom, and information, and trust your experience with people. If someone is destructive or producing bad fruit in your life, be careful. Keep looking, praying, and seeking until you find safe people—people who will give you all the benefits that God has planned for you (p. 168).

— *Prayer* —

Father God, thank you for this chapter and the hope you've kindled in me that there really are safe people out there. I understand that there are wolves—hurtful, destructive people—even in your family. But I believe that there are safe people, too, people whom you can use as channels of your love and healing. Thank you for specific ideas about where to find them. I ask that, as I look for a safe church, intimate friendships, a support group, and/or a therapist, you will grant me wisdom and discernment. Please keep me aware of when my character problems, my hurts, and my needs are interfering with my efforts to discern safe and unsafe people. Please, God, be with me as I practice what I've learned. I pray in Jesus' name. Amen.

CHAPTER TWELVE

Learning How to Be Safe

Have you wondered what you would do once you identified a safe person?

There are several major tasks and opportunities ahead of you after you have made the connection. Let's take a look at what you need to do to be safe. These efforts will lead you into deeper connections with God's people, which will then sustain you for life and growth (p. 169).

LEARN TO ASK FOR HELP

It isn't easy to ask for help, and it's risky. Yet it's absolutely the first key in having our safe people help nourish and mature us. In her counseling group, Stacy began to understand how terrified she was of allowing people who could give to her to get inside her (pp. 169–70).

* Where, if at all, do you see yourself in the description of Stacy? Do you need to tell someone that you're empty inside, that you have weaknesses and insecurities, and that you want him or her to tell you that he or she cares about you even when you're weak? Be specific about what's holding you back.

* If you've taken the risky and difficult step of finally asking for help, what happened? What did you learn? What did you let yourself receive from the person(s) who offered their help?

God places a high premium on the value of asking directly for help. Forms of the word "ask" appear almost eight hundred times in the Bible, many of them an invitation from God for us to ask for things (p. 170).

- What are some of the things God invites us to ask for? See Matthew 21:22, James 4:2, and 1 John 3:22.

- Talk about how difficult—or easy—it is for you to ask God for things, even when he extends the invitation. Why is asking difficult?

Learning to ask for love is important—and here are a few reasons why (p. 171).

1. When we ask, we develop humility (p. 171).

- Why is humility important to our spiritual health and growth?

- What things that you've had to ask for—or that you need to ask for today—have especially helped you develop humility?

2. When we ask, we are owning our needs (p. 171).

- What does it mean to "own our needs"?

- How does taking responsibility for our needs allow others to love us? How does owning our needs keep us from demanding love?

3. When we ask, we are taking initiative (p. 171).

- Why is asking the ultimate "Passivity-Buster"?

- Explain how asking keeps us much more in healthy control of our lives.

4. When we ask, we are developing a grateful character (p. 171).

- Explain the connection between asking and gratitude.

- Now explain the connection between asking, gratitude, and the kind of love God wants to have characterize his people (Luke 7:47).

5. Asking increases the odds that we'll get something (p. 172).

- When has not asking cost you? Put differently, who may not be in your life now because you didn't reach out and ask for something you needed?

- When has asking and being able to receive strengthened a relationship?

Asking is important—but what do we ask for? Asking for functional reasons (borrowing a cup of sugar or getting a ride to the airport) is fine, but that doesn't help develop relationships (p. 172).

- Asking for a functional reason may be a difficult enough first step for you. What practical help do you need? Whom will you ask? What will you say? Now ask! Let this be a practice run for asking for a relational need to be met.

- What relational need did Jesus ask his friends to meet in Gethsemane (see Mark 14:34)?

- What relational (spiritual and emotional, not merely physical) needs would you like to be able to ask someone to help meet?

- See on page 172 the list of possible ways to ask for a relational connection. Which way of asking, perhaps with a little tweaking, could you be comfortable saying? Now whom will you ask—and when?

LEARN TO NEED

Like the patients in the Bronx "Garden," those of us who have been emotionally detached may also have lost our ability to connect to the outside world. Our needs sleep within us. A genuine sense of rich connection to others is absent (p. 173).

Take a moment now to evaluate your ability to feel need.

• When have unmet needs caused you real hurt?

• How long have you been disconnected from real relationships?

• Does something inside you resonate when you read, "You may have been hurt, deprived, or disconnected from relationship for so long that the need simply died, leaving you with no experience of 'wanting' connection"? If so, learning to need is vital for you, for God created you to long for attachment. He designed your needs to tell you when you're on "empty."

You can regain your experience of neediness. After all, God is in the business of redeeming that which is lost, including disenfranchised parts of our soul (p. 174).

1. Confess your inability to need (p. 174).

• When has admitting that something is hard for you been freeing and made that something easier to do? Be specific—and know that the same principle works when it comes to admitting our inability to need.

• How would you, in your best safe person manner, respond to someone who let you know that he or she struggles to rely or depend on others, and actually wants others close, that he or she truly needs to need but isn't sure how? Know that a safe person will react that way to your confession—and your internal need will begin to respond to the warmth, constancy, and safety of that relationship.

2. Don't fake it (p. 174).

- Why is faking neediness and closeness harmful, not helpful, to the lost part of you?

- Safe people understand that healing past relational hurts and developing relationships take time. How can the lost part of you benefit from taking time and not trying to rush the process?

3. Keep your boundaries (pp. 174–75).

- Why can we be tempted to compromise our boundaries when we're learning to need? What harm can result?

- How will you let people know when you've had enough connecting time? Practice saying those words out loud so you'll have them ready when you need to feel safer.

4. Confess the need that you can't experience (p. 175).

- What need—one that you may not yet be experiencing—would you like to be able to share with someone? See the list on page 175 for some possibilities.

- Not being able to feel truths (like those truths in the list you just read) doesn't mean they're less true. How does this fact relate to your faith in God? To the process of learning to need?

5. Pay attention to what evokes your hunger (pp. 175–76).

- Why does it make sense that, after a certain amount of working on learning to need with safe people, your needs will awaken?

- Whenever you do sense that you've responded internally to a person, note what it was about what they said or did and how that relates to their character. Will you now tell that person — and this may not be easy — what it was about them that you were drawn to, how it helped you, and — it gets harder! — that you want more of that? You'll both benefit from such a statement: you'll get what you need and your friend will feel affirmed and needed.

WORK THROUGH RESISTANCE

Remember Tom's unusual "invitation" to form a home Bible study group that, in addition to learning content, doctrine, and application, would also learn about bonding? When he told the people gathered in his living room how much he didn't want such a group, Tom was normalizing resistance. Resistance is our tendency to avoid growth. It's our drive to keep the spiritual and emotional status quo. It's our inclination to move away from God's provisions for our growth (Rom. 7:15) — and we all have resistance (pp. 176–77).

- What spiritual and emotional growth are you especially resistant to?

- Many of the dynamics that drive us to choose unsafe people or no people (discussed in chapters 6, 7, and 8) are resistances—ways we keep our hearts from encountering loving, supportive people. What have you learned about your resistances to people who would help fill you up? Be specific—and beware of the attitude that you have no impediments to intimacy (1 Cor. 10:12). Accept the reality of your resistances or you'll lose out (Matt. 21:28–32).

In chapters 6, 7, and 8, we've listed how-to's for dealing with several important resistances to relationships. But here's a bird's-eye view of how to approach resistances (p. 177):

1. Identify your resistances (pp. 177–78).

- The more aware you are of your specific resistances to love, the more power you have over them. What do you do to keep yourself from encountering loving, supportive people? Make a list. A quick review of chapters 6, 7, and 8 may help.

- Get feedback from friends. What resistances do they see in you? What ways do they see you shrinking from safe people? Learn from what your friends tell you.

2. Bring them into relationship (p. 178).

- Why is it important to bring resistances into relationship not as an aside but as a focal point? What can happen when we do so?

- How will safe people respond to you when you share your resistances? Why will they respond that way? What do they know about themselves?

3. Meet the needs underlying the resistances (p. 178).

- Why did these oppositions originally arise? What were they designed to do for you?

- What will meeting your spiritual needs do to these resistances you developed as a means of self-protection?

4. Do the opposite of what the resistances tell you (pp. 178–79).

- Which destructive statements (listed on p. 178 of the text) have run through your mind during your efforts to learn to have people meet your emotional and relational needs?

- Why will rebelling against these voices and doing the exact opposite of what these resistances tell you serve you well?

INVITE THE TRUTH ABOUT YOURSELF

One of the most valuable things you can do with your safe people—ranking right up there with asking for help, needing, and melting resistance—is simply to invite the truth about yourself. God often uses people to answer our prayer that he reveal to us our blindspots about ourselves (Ps. 139:23–24). Regularly asking two questions of your safe people—"What do I do that pushes you away from me?" and "What do I do that draws you toward me?"—can help you learn much about yourself and love, limits, goodness, badness, and relationships (pp. 179–80).

• What was your initial reaction to those two questions and the thought of asking them?

• How could a person—how could you—benefit from the insights, perceptions, emotions, and observations these two questions can prompt?

• Who will be the first person you ask these questions? When will you do so?

Although you may know when and with whom you want to raise these two questions, you may still be nervous—even terrified—by the prospect. Know that, unlike people you may have encountered in the past, safe people won't be hurtful or share untrue things; they're not waiting to pounce on you. Your safe person wants you to know the truth for two reasons (p. 180).

• First, the truth increases love. Explain why. You might refer to 1 John 4:18.

- Second, the truth is always your friend. Why is the truth a friend? See John 8:32. From what can the truth set you free?

- As you ask the safe people in your life these two questions, keep a journal about what you learn about yourself. What truths that they speak help you accept yourself and be more open about who you are? What truths show you changes you can make in order to improve your relationships? Note, too, any loving, affirming statements made to you and about you in the past that have been tools of healing.

ENTER INTO FORGIVENESS

One of the greatest benefits you'll find in your safe settings is a deepening understanding of failure and what to do with it. And the key to dealing with failure is always forgiveness.

When the Jiminy Cricket voice prompted me (John) to call Ken, I learned from him that he had truly forgiven me for the way I'd hurt him years ago (pp. 181–82).

- What have the Kens in your life taught you about forgiveness?

- Are you a Ken, able to forgive and move on, able to let go of the past and invest your energy in the rest of the relationship? To whom could you be a Ken? When you truly let go of the hurt in the past, you'll be freeing yourself from it, too.

Safe people are forgiving people for several reasons. First, they know that they continually need divine and human "debt-cancellations." They also expect failure and disappointment from those they love. And, like Jesus (Isa. 53:3), they are familiar with the losses and sins of this post-Fall, pre-eternity world. Finally, they know that loving is much more important than holding onto the past, as long as the past has been worked through and resolved (pp. 182–83).

- Where do you see yourself in this description of safe people and their attitude toward forgiveness?

- Where do you see a need to grow into a safer, more forgiving person?

You can learn to be a safer, more forgiving person by sharpening the two skills of forgiveness (p. 183).

1. Learn to receive forgiveness (p. 183).

- When has someone extended forgiveness to you? What did it feel like to be known but not condemned?

- Explain how receiving forgiveness can help us accept the realities—the bad as well as the good—of who we are.

- Review the list of skills involved in receiving forgiveness (p. 183). Which ones do you need to work on? Which will you choose to tackle first? When and with whom will you practice that skill?

2. Learn to give forgiveness (pp. 183–84).

- Why does it make sense that forgiven people become forgiving people?

- How does holding on to the hurts of others, awaiting either justice or an apology, keep us unable to love other people? Why does it make us less able to take in the freedom that comes with forgiving? Let your answers to these questions help you explain how giving forgiveness frees you at a deeper level than it frees the perpetrator.

- Now review the list of things to do with your safe people that will help you become more forgiving (p. 184). Which activities do you need to work on? Which will you choose to tackle first? When and with whom will you take that step?

GIVE SOMETHING BACK

We've looked at the five emotional and spiritual character growth tasks that safe relationships were made for, tasks that we are to accomplish so that we who were "created in Christ Jesus to do good works" (Eph. 2:10) can indeed do so. As we receive all the goodness that comes from doing these tasks and letting ourselves be helped by safe people, gratitude takes over, and we feel a responsibility to give to others what we've taken in. We want to give something back.

Maybe, however, you don't feel grateful. If not, make that an issue to explore. Are you new to this process and, like a newborn baby, still in a major "receiving" stage (1 Peter 2:2)? Or have you not really allowed love to sink in? Or are you devaluing the love people are offering you? Investigate why you aren't yet feeling grateful.

If you are feeling gratitude for all the goodness you've been receiving, here are some principles to guide you as you consider where, when, and how you can give something back (p. 185).

1. Understand what you've gained (pp. 185–86).

- Make a list of what you've learned about spiritual and emotional dynamics, about relationships, about God, and about yourself. Have you learned about whom you can trust, that your needs are okay, how to be honest, or when you withdraw? Be specific.

- What does your list suggest about what you can give back?

2. Learn your friends' "need signals" (p. 186).

- Think of a close friend. What specific "need signals" does he or she send out? How do you know when that person is in need?

- If you were unable to answer the previous question, what does this show you about yourself? What will you do to learn your friends' "need signals"?

3. Ask to help (p. 186).

- How would you respond to someone saying, "You've meant a lot to me. Help me know what you need and what part I can play with my own resources"? How would you feel?

- Make that statement an offer of help you can extend to the safe people in your life. What words will you feel comfortable saying to one of your safe people who is in need?

4. Be there (p. 186).

- When has someone loved you by doing? When has someone loved you by being there — by listening to your pain and sitting with you while you hurt? Compare the two incidents and the different impact they had on you.

- Do you have an easier time "loving by doing" than "loving by being there" or "loving by being 'Jesus in the flesh,'" as God calls us to be? Why do you struggle to simply be there with someone who is hurting? Make your discomfort with quietness, pain, or tears — whatever the barrier — a topic of prayer. Ask God to enable you to overcome it so that you can be there for the safe people who have been there for you.

5. Tell the truth (p. 186).

- Why is it important — even though it is often difficult — to tell your safe people when they are hurting you, themselves, or others? How can they benefit from your loving and humble confrontation?

- What can you do to avoid sounding parental when you confront? What knowledge of yourself will keep you humble?

6. Go into the world (pp. 186–87).

- For whom outside of your "safety zone" can you become a safe person? Consider the lonely, the oppressed, and the less fortunate—people who have absolutely nothing to offer you in return. Consider, too, non-Christians, minorities, single-parent families, substance abusing people in recovery, those with emotional struggles, AIDS victims, mission organizations, and your neighbors. In what direction is God nudging you to get involved?

- Why is it important to go into the world with the safety you have received and learned to offer others? Consider, for instance, Jesus' words in Matthew 28:18–20.

To become a safe person, you need to practice over and over again the six steps we've looked at—asking for help, learning to need, working through resistances, inviting the truth about yourself, entering into forgiveness, and giving something back. Know that this ongoing work will reap wonderful spiritual and emotional fruit for you and for others (p. 187).

— *Prayer* —

Father God, thank you for what you've shown me about how I can be a safe person. The tasks—asking for help, learning to need, working through resistances, inviting the truth about myself, entering into forgiveness, and giving something back—would sound quite overwhelming if it weren't for my knowledge of your presence with me in the process, and if it weren't for the safe people you have brought and are bringing into my life to model these things for me.

As I work on these tasks, Lord, keep me humble and teachable. Give me courage to take new steps and new risks. Please continue to offer your support through your people. And please continue to use them to help me become more the person you want me to be.

Then, Lord, as I give back from what you have given me through your safe people, use me for your kingdom. I thank you for the taste of your kingdom that safe people give me—and I thank you for the privilege of being used by you. I pray in Jesus' name. Amen.

CHAPTER THIRTEEN

Should I Repair or Replace?

The chief theme of the Bible—and of our teaching—is reconciliation of unsafe re-lationships. This call to reconciliation means that no relationship can be left without a struggle to negotiate and resolve problems. This biblical approach is a far cry from the easy out that says, "When I realized this person was unsafe, I left him."

The Bible shows that God didn't—and still doesn't—move away from relationships with unsafe people. Instead, he moved toward the relationship and became a facilitator of healing—and we are to learn from and follow his example (p. 189).

- What happened in the Garden (Gen. 3:1–7) that broke humankind's relationship with God? Did God keep the people who had hurt him (Ezek. 6:9) or did he move on? Describe his actions.

- How do you react when the relationship you had in mind is broken? What emotions and thoughts do you experience?

- On what basis do you decide whether to try to keep the relationship or to move on?

THE CHALLENGE OF REPAIRING A RELATIONSHIP

Our battle with feelings of hurt, revenge, forgiveness, compassion, and grief that we even entered into the relationship at all, rages as we try to decide whether to reconcile and work things out or whether to count the relationship as a loss and move on. When we are at such a crossroads, it is helpful to remember how God handled the problem of difficult relationships. Looking to him as our model, we find six steps we can take in our own difficult relationships (p. 190).

1. Start from a loved position.

In order to work out a difficult relationship, we need to be secure in our other relationships (John 17:24). If we aren't and if we feel that we need any one person in order to survive, we will not be able to resolve the relationship. Our dependency keeps us from being ourselves and doing the right thing (pp. 190–91).

• When has your dependency on a person kept you in an unhealthy, unsafe relationship with him or her? Explain the circumstances.

• When has your human need for relationship with others led you to compromise your values?

• When has a strong support system enabled you, as it did Debbie, to take a stand in a relationship? What about the support made you finally feel ready and able to confront the unsafe person?

• Evaluate your support system as it exists today. Is it strong enough to help you deal with a current difficult relationship? If so, what step will you take in that relationship? If not, what will you do to strengthen your support system?

2. Act righteously.

Always doing the right thing comes easily for God, but it is difficult for us—especially because we'd rather not have to change when we are part of the problem. While it would be easier to avoid making such painful and difficult changes in ourselves, that kind of laziness never accomplishes our wish to have good relationships. Furthermore, unless we do that work, we continue to return evil for evil (Rom. 12:17) and remain part of the destructive pattern (p. 192).

•   Debbie had some weaknesses she had to face before the relationship with her husband could change. What weaknesses (fear of aloneness, fear of conflict, a tendency to keep up the facade of a perfect family, not opening up to friends for support and help, etc.) do you bring into relationships?

•   In order to have safe people in our lives, we must first become safe people ourselves. Explain why changing our own character first is a key.

•   Which of the weaknesses you identified above are playing into an unsafe relationship in which you are currently struggling? What work does resolving those weaknesses demand? What steps are you taking to do so—or what's keeping you from getting to work?

3. Use others to help.

When God is working in a person's life, he does not do so by himself—he uses the community around the problem person. He uses people to confront, discipline, guide, and lead the people he's trying to change (pp. 192–93).

•   Read Matthew 18:15–20. What instructions do you find here for how God wants us to be used in other people's lives so that he can confront, discipline, guide, lead, and ultimately change them?

- When has God used you to intervene in someone's life so that he could work to heal and change that person? Or when has God used people to intervene in your life to move you to receive the healing help you needed? Describe the emotions, process, and outcome of either event.

- When has God used safe people to provide you with wisdom and knowledge for dealing with a problem individual (Prov. 11:14)? Be specific about the lessons you learned.

- Do you need to turn to the community for help with an unhealthy, unsafe relationship? What will be your first step?

4. Accept reality, forgive, and grieve your expectations.

God accepts us as we are even though we are far from what he wants us to be. He has given up the ideal, grieved that loss, and decided to love us anyway. He has accepted reality because he wants relationship. To do that takes forgiveness and acceptance, a giving up of the way things "should" be (Col. 2:13–14), and accepting things the way they are (pp. 193–95).

- *God's acceptance doesn't mean he lets our faults slide. He loves us too much for that. But it does mean that he isn't condemning and angry, shaming or vengeful, judgmental or punitive. He wants to deal with things that get in the way of our relationships with him and with each other (p. 194).* How do you tend to deal with the faults, real or perceived, in problem people? What does God's example suggest about changes you need to make in yourself?

- *In addition to not making us feel bad for our imperfections, God does not come to us with a list of expectations that do not fit who we are (p. 194).* Think about your primary unsafe person. Are you concerned about sin in that person's life or are you criticizing aspects of his or her basic personhood rather than enjoying the unique person God has created?

- We need to give up our expectations for people to be faultless or to be different from who they really are. What does this truth tell you about your perspective on the problem people in your life? What changes do you need to make in yourself and your expectations? Which of your own perfectionistic expectations and demands may be causing the conflicts? Whom do you need to work on forgiving as God forgave you? Whose God-given uniqueness do you need to learn to enjoy?

5. Give change a chance.

Many times people will get tired of what they've been putting up with in a relationship and finally "get some boundaries." Then their first exercise of these boundaries, they think, is leaving the relationship. That, however, is a cop-out. A person with true boundaries would go back into the relationship and take stands on the individual problems that come up day by day. This is the true test of boundaries: to be in the relationship and not be controlled or abused. Facing up to a difficult relationship is the only guarantee that you will learn and be able to do the right thing in a new relationship (pp. 195–96).

- When have you "gotten boundaries" and left a relationship? What regrets do you have? What lessons did you learn? Did any growth result from leaving the fire of the relationship?

- When have you "gotten boundaries" and then endured the real test of your newly-defined character and stayed in the relationship? What lessons did you learn? What genuine growth has resulted?

- We never really know if the relationship has a chance until we begin to do the right thing over time. When have someone's efforts to make some character changes helped turn around a friendship, business relationship, family relationship, marriage, or dating relationship? When have your efforts to change your character forced change in another person and thereby turned around a difficult situation?

6. Be long-suffering.

Exodus 34:6–7 describes God as "the compassionate and gracious God, slow to anger, abounding in love and faithfulness, maintaining love to thousands, and forgiving wickedness, rebellion and sin." God tries for a long time to work out a relationship with each one of us, and he is ready to forgive when people own their part in the problem. Clearly, God is not one who gives up on relationship easily, and we are to model this character trait as well (pp. 196–97).

- When have you seen compassion, grace, slowness to anger, and an abundance of love and faithfulness pay off in a relationship? Talk from your personal experience or share an example of long-suffering that you have seen.

- But how long is too long to hang in with a difficult person? Only you and God know—but it's usually longer than you think! It's past the point of pain, past the point of revenge, past the point of despair, as God gives us the supernatural ability to love and keep seeking an answer. What is God saying to you and even convicting you about in these truths? What relationship may he be calling you to continue in? Make that relationship the focus of a few minutes of silent prayer right now.

SEPARATION: THE FINAL OPTION

Despite God's call to us to be long-suffering in relationships as he is, there are times when we have done all we can do. We've given the relationship time and opened ourselves up to trying to reconcile, yet the person is unwilling to face his or her part. Reconciliation and change do not occur. We can still forgive, but we cannot reconcile without the other person's willingness. The Bible then tells us to separate (Matt. 18:17; 1 Cor. 5:9–12), but we must be open to the person's later repentance (Luke 17:3–4) and restoration of the relationship in the future. Sometimes separation is necessary, but often it is not permanent.

When we separate, we are not rejecting a person; he or she is rejecting a relationship with us. For example, a wife takes a stand for fidelity. If her husband wants to be with her, he must remain faithful. She is not rejecting him if he chooses to be unfaithful; he is rejecting her values (p. 197).

- If you are feeling the need to separate, what will you do to communicate clearly that you are not rejecting the person?

- When have you seen—in your life or that of another person—separation being necessary but not permanent? What healing did God do in the two people's lives once the separation occurred?

Even when we have no other choice but to give up a destructive relationship, we will feel a loss—and we need to let ourselves face that loss and feel the sadness (pp. 197–98).

- What can happen if we don't adequately face the loss? What aspects of our history would we have a tendency to repeat?

- To have something new, we must first lose the old. What grieving do you need to do for lost relationships? How will you proceed?

A WORD ABOUT DIVORCE

We believe that the Bible teaches that marriage is permanent and is to be worked out. We also believe that divorce is permissible in certain circumstances—adultery or desertion by an unbelieving spouse (Matt. 5:31–32; 1 Cor. 7:15)—but God's ideal is for even those circumstances to be redeemed. That does not mean, however, that someone in a destructive, abusive situation is obliged to remain passive and be hurt (p. 198).

- If you are in a difficult marriage, have you begun to work through the six steps outlined in this chapter? Do so prayerfully, diligently, and with the support of people who love you—and start today.

- If you have been divorced, do you rest in God's gracious forgiveness and acceptance? Do you believe in his unconditional love for you and his desire to take your brokenness and redeem it? If you struggle with these things, talk to God and your safe people about it. Let God's people give you a taste of his unconditional love. Let him use them as vessels of hope and healing in your life.

HOW LONG IS LONG ENOUGH?

So when do we repair, and when do we replace? There is no clear-cut answer. Long-suffering is, by definition, long. Look again at page 199 of the text and the list of guidelines designed to help you know when you are not ready to replace a significant relationship (pp. 198–99).

• What does this list tell you about the next step you need to take in the significant relationship you are struggling with?

• The guidelines you've just looked at hurt; they take time and a lot of effort. But relationships are the most important aspect of the spiritual life. In fact, they are the spiritual life, as God defines it. Explain what that last statement means (Matt. 22:35–40 may help).

• Romans 12:18 reads, "If it is possible, as far as it depends on you, live at peace with everyone." What answer to the question "How long is long enough?" does this verse provide?

• What is God saying to you through this verse about the difficult relationship you are struggling with most? Again, only you and God can know how long is too long to hang in with a difficult person.

The message of this book is a lot like the message of the gospel. It has good news and bad news. The good news is that you can be saved from a life of relational hell with unsafe people. The bad news is that you must take up your cross and do the hard work of dealing with your own character problems.

We have found in our lives and in the lives of others that the process outlined here works. If you will do the hard work of distinguishing safe and unsafe people, abiding deeply with the safe ones and dealing redemptively with the unsafe ones, you will develop an abundant life, full of satisfying relationships and meaningful service to God (p. 199).

— *Prayer* —

Father God, thank you for the message of this book. Thank you for its good news—that I don't have to live a life of relational hell with unsafe people. And thank you that even its bad news—that I must take up my cross and do the hard work of dealing with my own character problems—is good news in that it points me to the path of healing, wholeness, and the freedom to enjoy relationships as you intend them to be.

Lord, I thank you for the safe people you've already brought into my life and ask that you would continue to bless me with people who can help me become the person you want me to be. I also pray that you will continue to work in me to make me a safe person for others.

Also, please guide me as I seek to deal redemptively with the unsafe people now in my life and any I may encounter in the future. And, Lord, use me—and all that I've learned and all that you'll continue to teach me—in your kingdom and for your glory. I pray in Jesus' name. Amen.

EMBARK ON A
LIFE-CHANGING JOURNEY
OF PERSONAL AND SPIRITUAL GROWTH

DR. HENRY CLOUD

DR. JOHN TOWNSEND

Dr. Henry Cloud and Dr. John Townsend have been bringing hope and healing to millions for over two decades. They have helped people everywhere discover solutions to life's most difficult personal and relational challenges. Their material provides solid, practical answers and offers guidance in the areas of *parenting, singles issues, personal growth,* and *leadership*.

Bring either Dr. Cloud or Dr. Townsend to your church or organization. They are available for:

- Seminars on a wide variety of topics
- Training for small group leaders
- Conferences
- Educational events
- Consulting with your organization

Other opportunities to experience Dr. Cloud and Dr. Townsend:

- Ultimate Leadership workshops—held in Southern California throughout the year
- Small group curriculum
- Seminars via Satellite
- Solutions Audio Club—Solutions is a weekly recorded presentation

For other resources, and for dates of seminars and workshops
by Dr. Cloud and Dr. Townsend, visit:
www.cloudtownsend.com

For other information **Call (800) 676-HOPE (4673)**

Or write to:
Cloud-Townsend Resources
18092 Sky Park South, Suite A
Irvine, CA 92614

Boundaries Updated and Expanded Edition

When to Say Yes, How to Say No To Take Control of Your Life

Dr. Henry Cloud and Dr. John Townsend

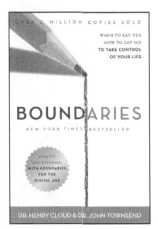

Boundaries is the book that's helped over 2 million people learn when to say yes and know how to say no in order to take control of their lives.

Does your life feel like it's out of control? Perhaps you feel like you have to say yes to everyone's requests. Maybe you find yourself readily taking responsibility for others' feelings and problems. Or perhaps you focus so much on being loving and unselfish that you've forgotten your own limits and limitations. Or maybe it's all of the above.

In the New York Times bestseller, *Boundaries*, Drs. Henry Cloud and John Townsend help you learn when to say yes and know how to say no in order to take control of your life and set healthy, biblical boundaries with your spouse, children, friends, parents, co-workers, and even yourself.

Now updated and expanded for the digital age, this book continues to help millions of people around the world answer these tough questions:

- Can I set limits and still be a loving person?
- What are legitimate boundaries?
- How do I effectively manage my digital life so that it doesn't control me?
- What if someone is upset or hurt by my boundaries?
- How do I answer someone who wants my time, love, energy, or money?
- Why do I feel guilty or afraid when I consider setting boundaries?
- How do boundaries relate to mutual submission within marriage?
- Aren't boundaries selfish?

You don't have to let your life spiral out of control. Discover how boundaries make life better today!

Plus, check out Boundaries family collection of books dedicated to key areas of life—dating, marriage, raising kids, parenting teens, and leadership. Workbooks and Spanish editions are also available.

Available in stores and online!